Restoring Joy

Elizabeth J. Davis

Printed in the United States of America

ISBN: 9798840752999

10 9 8 7 6 5 4 3 2 1

EMPIRE PUBLISHING
www.empirebookpublishing.com

Table of Contents

Thank you to my pastors, the Reverends Roger and Kim Wood, for their direction, encouragement, and assistance throughout the writing of this book.

Forward

When I was a teenager, my pastor at that time said to me, "Elizabeth, one day you will write a book." I envisioned an exciting fiction book! Maybe I would author many wholesome fictional books like LaJoyce Martin.

Years later after a prayer meeting, God impressed upon my current First Lady to say, "Elizabeth, you should write a book on joy."

I looked back at her in astonishment. Really? Aren't there hundreds of books on this subject? What am I supposed to write about joy?

A few days later, I was praying in my home and asking God the above questions. The Holy Spirit impressed me, "Get a paper and pen." I obeyed and, immediately, ideas and inspirations flowed and I wrote as fast as I could.

Then, "Lord, why me?" Why choose me to write this? There are definitely people more qualified and educated. I have finally decided He chose me to write it because I need it the most. I smile as I write this but I am sure it is true.

While praying at home one evening, the majority of my church family was at an out-of-town multi-church gathering. I was unable to attend due to my work schedule. I had yet to begin the writing of this book. God's still small voice spoke clearly into my mind, "Restoring Joy." Instantly, I felt He had given me the title. When I asked a friend about the minister's message, they said the title of his sermon was "Restore" – my confirmation.

I finally approached my First Lady that I was officially beginning to write this book. The day I approached her, she had just had a dream where God had revealed to her that there were a certain number of people He was moving on to author books.

I got rolling with the writing then ran out of steam. Life got "busy." I could not seem to "get around" to finishing the book.

Then, a missionary came and preached a simple but powerful message on being obedient and doing what God asks us to do. As I knelt at the altar in response to the preached word, God clearly spoke into my mind, "You haven't finished the book I told you to write."

I felt like I needed another resource to draw from on joy. As my pastor preached a series of messages on joy, he referred to the book "Better Than Medicine: A Merry Heart" by Leroy Brownlow saying it was an excellent book. I got on Amazon and searched for the cheapest copy I could find. I did not care about the quality, I just wanted it for a reference. I ordered one that said it had some writing on the inside cover but, otherwise, was in good condition. When I received it in the mail, the book was in perfect condition. The writing on the inside cover gave me pause—"Elizabeth Davis." Evidently, this copy had been gifted to someone with my exact name in 1985. What a confirmation that I was on the right track!

I just want to be God's conduit. My prayer is that He will write through me.

This book on joy is not comprehensive but it is what God has given me. Each chapter could become a book in itself with further indepth study.

I am a note taker as will be evidenced by references to various speakers and teachers throughout this book from whom I have gleaned much wisdom.

I pray that as you begin to read this book that your heart is open to whatever God desires to speak to you as an individual. Do not immediately dismiss any of its content but be prayerful and verify what is being said with His Word.

Be willing to embrace what He speaks to you and walk in further revelation.

Psalm 119:30 says, "I have chosen the way of truth."

God's Word is truth. The treasures we discover as we walk with Him and learn from His Word are unending.

May God bless and enrich you through the content of this book and His Word which is frequently referenced throughout its pages.

Restoring Joy

1. Restore

"Pssst… Ethan. Ethan!"

"Ouch! Quit poking me, Simon!"

"I've been rattling my chains for the past five minutes and you've snored right through it. What do you need to wake you up? An earthquake?"

"I just want to go back to sleep," responded Ethan.

"Why? That's about all we do around here. I'm bored."

"You interrupted a good dream, Simon!"

"Ah ha! You were dreaming about Jemimah again, weren't you? Weren't you, Ethan? Ethan?"

A soft snore began to waft through the dark prison chamber. Simon grunted in frustration and tried again.

"Ethan!"

"Aaugh! Simon! You know, if you're going to try to really wake me up, brew some fresh coffee or something."

"As if I could. Don't you know what time it is?"

"No. Do you?"

"No idea in this constant darkness but I've got a feeling it's time to wake up. Besides, I've been thinking and remembering and if you don't wake up and listen my head might explode from all these thoughts!"

Ethan sighed in resignation, "Fine. I'll make you a deal."

"What?" Simon sounded hopeful.

"I'll wake up and talk if you let me share my dream first."

"If I hear one more dream about Jemim-"

"Aw, come on. It's not Jemimah this time, okay?"

"Hmm… then make it short," Simon grunted.

"Remember that old prophet, Isaiah?"

"How could I forget?"

4

"You know our parents didn't like him. Sometimes, they would listen to what he had to say but then they wouldn't do anything about it!"

"I remember, Ethan, because I was just thinking-"

"Wait! I'm not done yet," Ethan held up his hand. "I was dreaming of when we were back in Judah. Isaiah said God delights in us. He said our God created the heavens and spread forth the earth. Our God is the one who gives us our very breath! He is the only God and we are to sing to Him and praise Him."

"Interesting you would be dreaming this, Ethan, because-"

"Shhh... Isaiah said God would lead us in paths we had not known and make the crooked things straight. Isn't that amazing, Simon?"

"That's just what I wanted to talk about. See, I'm really troubled because Isaiah's prophecy has come true."

"Which one?" Ethan raised an eyebrow.

"I remember all those wonderful things Isaiah was saying but then he said, 'But this is a people robbed and spoiled; they are all of them snared in holes, and they are hid in prison houses: they are for a prey, and none delivereth; for a spoil, and none saith, Restore'' (Isaiah 42:22). Simon began to choke on silent sobs.

Ethan stared silently at his friend for a long moment then spoke, "I know, Bro. I know."

"We have been stuck in this dark old prison, and the prophecy has happened! According to what Isaiah said, there is no one to cry out on our behalf! There is none to advocate our restoration and let us return home."

"Simon, don't you remember more of what Isaiah spoke?"

This time, Simon raised an eyebrow, "Of course. He spoke enough to fill a book!"

Ethan actually chuckled.

"What are you laughing about? Don't you see we are in a hopeless situation?" Simon sighed.

"Your mind is so full of the negative that you haven't allowed room for the positive, my friend."

Simon fixed Ethan with an intense stare, "If you have something positive to tell me, hurry and do it before I go nuts!"

"We are not without hope. Reach way back into your memory and pull this out! After Isaiah spoke that prophecy, he said, 'But now thus saith the LORD that created thee, O Jacob, and he that formed thee, O Israel, Fear not: for I have redeemed thee, I have called thee by thy name; thou art mine."

"When thou passest through the waters, I will be with thee; and through the rivers, they shall not overflow thee: when thou walkest through the fire, thou shalt not be burned; neither shall the flame kindle upon thee."

"For I am the LORD thy God, the Holy One of Israel, thy Saviour: I gave Egypt for thy ransom, Ethiopia and Seba for thee."

"Since thou wast precious in my sight, thou hast been honourable, and I have loved thee: therefore will I give men for thee, and people for thy life."

"Fear not: for I am with thee…'"

Simon began to cut in, "'…I will bring thy seed from the east, and gather thee from the west;

"I will say to the north, Give up; and to the south, Keep not back: bring my sons from far, and my daughters from the ends of the earth;"

"Even every one that is called by my name: for I have created him for my glory, I have formed him; yea, I have made him."

Ethan rattled his chains in excitement, "You're getting it!"

Simon was sitting up straighter than he had in weeks with eyes bright, "Restoration is coming because God will bring it!"

"Right! I don't like how we got ourselves into this mess by not listening to God and not obeying His commands but He still loves us and will restore us. I've sure learned my lesson. Haven't you, Simon?"

6

Wherever you are in life and whatever your situation, there is hope for you! Consider that the children of Israel had backslidden from God. It was their own fault they were taken into captivity. It was a mess of their own making. Yet, God still promised restoration. He said He would gather them together again from every country back into the promised land.

Jeremiah 30:17 says, "For I will restore health unto thee, and I will heal thee of thy wounds, saith the LORD."

Furthermore, in Jeremiah 31:13 God said, "Then shall the virgin rejoice in the dance, both young men and old together: for I will turn their mourning into joy, and will comfort them, and make them rejoice from their sorrow."

However, sometimes we are doing all we know to do to live right before God. Then, a tragedy strikes leaving us feeling empty and void of joy. Or, maybe as we continue on life's path, we realize we ran out of joy along the way.

In this end time, the enemy is doing whatever he can to steal our joy. He wants to make our lives a drudgery. He wants to replace our joyful relationship with God with a day by day existence of going through the motions.

If he can accomplish this, we are in danger! Without joy, how can we show others the way? Without joy, how can we offer pure praise and worship to God? Without joy, how can we have the peace that passes all understanding?

The focus of this book is on restoring joy back into our lives through an ever deepening relationship with God. Our Maker Himself is calling for restoration of our joy in this end time! Let's get up and do something about it.

2. Joy Defined

What words can truly define joy? The Apostle Peter wrote of "joy unspeakable" (1 Peter 1:8).

When I was fourteen, I specifically remember a time when I was full of joy. I was involved in my local church, praying daily, and faithfully studying the Word of God. Plus, I had been to a Pentecostal youth camp and received a fresh baptism of the Holy Ghost. In Pentecost, we call it a "refilling."

Every moment of every day I was so full of praise and thanksgiving and happiness on the inside that I felt like I could explode. I constantly felt like I could just start running and not stop.

I cannot remember how long this continued until I finally told the Lord in prayer one day, "Lord, I'm so full of joy that I can't handle it." In response to my prayer, that feeling faded away.

My teenage mind perceived that time of exuberant energy and gladness from time with Him and being involved in His kingdom as joy.

One time I could not find my glasses. I searched and finally found them—on top of my head. They were there the whole time. I just did not feel them. Joy is not a feeling although our feelings can be influenced by our joy. Therefore, we cannot judge our joyfulness by our feelings just like we cannot judge our amount of joy by our circumstances. Joy is for all of the time—good and bad.

I did not lose my joy as a teenager. But, that particular feeling faded.

Joy is not a feeling. It does not come and go with the change of our mood. But, as we will see further in this chapter, the Bible describes joy in multiple ways.

Joy is a calm delight in God. Joy is also an exceeding gladness. Then, joy manifests as an exuberant rejoicing and shouting!

Think of a beautiful piece of music. The melody flows throughout the song. It may start soft and soothing followed by a crescendo into a boisterous, exciting climax! Then, it flows back to a gentle tune.

The same is true with joy. It flows throughout our lives constantly whether in times of calm delight in God or rapturous glee or shouting and dancing.

Joy does not just happen. We have to invite it! How? When you finish this book, you will have either learned or been reminded of several ways to invite then maintain true joy.

Joy is a choice. We must daily choose to operate in the joy of the Lord and learn how to exercise it and maintain it in our lives.

Let us pause and look at how the Holman Bible Dictionary defines joy. Joy is "the happy state that results from knowing and serving God." The synonyms it lists for joy are happiness, pleasure, delight, gladness, merriment, felicity, and enjoyment.

Truly, joy is a product of knowing and serving God!

Romans 14:17 says "the kingdom of God is… righteousness, and peace, and joy in the Holy Ghost." Joy is a product of the infilling of the Holy Ghost!

If you have witnessed someone being filled with the Holy Ghost evidenced by speaking in other tongues, words cannot describe the radiant glow of joy on their face! When I received His Spirit as a child, I still remember the abundant joy I felt.

But Romans 14:17 does not say it is for when you are first filled with the Holy Ghost only, it is a continuing product of someone who is filled with God's Spirit. Hallelujah! This leads us to the next point.

Joy is a fruit of the Spirit. The Holy Ghost literally produces fruit in the life of a Spirit-filled believer! Galatians 5:22-23 gives us a list of these spiritual fruits, "But the fruit of the Spirit is love, joy, peace, longsuffering, gentleness, goodness, faith, meekness, temperance: against such there is no law."

Along with eight other wonderful fruits is joy! Don't we serve such a wonderful God? He gives us such a well-rounded group of fruits to help us as we serve Him.

Compare the above list to the works of the flesh listed in the previous verses, "Now the works of the flesh are manifest, which are these; Adultery, fornication, uncleanness, lasciviousness,

Idolatry, witchcraft, hatred, variance, emulations, wrath, strife, seditions, heresies,

Envyings, murders, drunkenness, revellings, and such like: of the which I tell you before, as I have also told you in time past, that they which do such things shall not inherit the kingdom of God" (Galatians 5:19-21).

I want to choose the fruit of the Spirit! Don't you?

Let us take a moment to familiarize ourselves with the Biblical meanings of the word joy.

The word joy as used in Galatians 5:22 comes from the Greek word "chara" which means "cheerfulness, calm delight, gladness." Other examples of when this word for joy is used is when Jesus endured the cross for the joy that was set before Him (Hebrews 12:2), when the wise men saw the star that led them to Jesus (Matthew 2:10), the discovery of the kingdom of heaven (Matthew 13:44), rejoicing and leaping for joy over our reward in Heaven (Luke 6:23), and many more!

In the Old Testament, the Hebrew word "simchah" means "blithesomeness or glee, exceeding gladness, joyfulness, mirth, pleasure, rejoicing." A few ways this meaning of joy is used is when worshiping God with musical instruments (1 Kings 1:40), eating and celebrating (Nehemiah 8:10 & Esther 9:22), lifting your voice in worship and singing (1 Chronicles 15:16), giving into the Kingdom of God (1 Chronicles 29:9), victory over enemies (Esther 8:16-17, 2 Chronicles 20:27), and being in God's presence (Psalm 16:11).

Another Hebrew word for joy is "teruw'ah." This means "clamor, acclamation of joy or battle-cry, clangor of trumpets as an alarm, jubilee, loud noise, rejoicing, shouting." A few examples of its usages include seeing God's face (Job 33:26), singing to God (Psalm 27:6), and when God's joy comes after a time of mourning (Psalm 30:5).

The mere study of the definition and usages of joy is a book of its own. Hopefully, the above references will whet your appetite into the wondrous indepth study of this delightful topic.

The best definition of joy can be summarized in one sentence. Joy is God! Or, God is joy! All that joy is can be found in Him. Without Him, you have no joy. You may experience happiness or pleasure for brief periods of time but when it ends, you are empty.

The Declaration of Independence says that all men are "endowed by their Creator with certain unalienable Rights, that among these are Life, Liberty and the pursuit of Happiness." Unfortunately, people pursue happiness and miss finding true joy and fulfillment. The result? Emptiness.

Colossians 2:10 says, "And ye are complete in him, which is the head of all principality and power."

When we pursue Jesus, we obtain joy! We find completeness in Him!

3. Further Revelation Brings Joy

The sun beamed down on Philip as he trudged through the desert. He had recently preached in Samaria and had baptized many in Jesus' name and seen them receive the Holy Ghost. As a result, "there was great joy in that city" (Acts 8:8). What an amazing work the Lord was doing in Samaria!

Why did the Lord direct him to go for a walk in the desert between Jerusalem and Gaza? He did not know the reason yet but he did know he was in the will of God.

What was that in the distance? He rubbed the dust out of his eyes and blinked just to be sure it was not a mirage. No, it was not his imagination. In the distance was a fellow traveler in a chariot. A chariot! It sure would be nice to hitch a ride and get off his aching feet.

Then Philip heard the voice of the Lord, "Go near, and join thyself to this chariot."

Without hesitation, he forgot his aching feet and began to run. As he drew near, he noticed the man in the chariot was an Ethiopian of obvious wealth and authority.

"Did I put on deodorant this morning? I know my teeth are brushed but that was a while ago. I dressed to walk in the desert — not meet a government official!" If these thoughts ran through Philip's mind, he did not let them delay his obedience in approaching this man.

However, the man did not immediately look up. He was engrossed in reading something out loud.

"I would want a good read if I had to ride for hours through this desert," Philip may have thought. He strained his ears to hear what the man was reading as he drew even closer.

"He was led as a sheep to the slaughter; and like a lamb dumb before his shearer, so opened he not his mouth:

In his humiliation his judgment was taken away: and who shall declare his generation? For his life is taken from the earth," the Ethiopian read.

"Wow! He is reading from the book of Isaiah the prophet! Okay, Lord, this is definitely a divine encounter!" Philip mused. Then he raised his voice and asked, "Do you understand what you are reading?"

The man raised his head and their gazes locked. "How can I, except some man should guide me? Please, Sir, join me."

"Hallelujah!" Philip thought to himself as he climbed in and sat down.

The Ethiopian lifted the pages of Isaiah and pointed to where he was reading, "I pray thee, of whom speaketh the prophet this? Of himself, or of some other man?"

The Bible tells us this man was a eunuch of great authority under Candace, queen of the Ethiopians. He had charge of all her treasure. Yet, he took the time to travel to Jerusalem to worship. He studied the Scriptures. Obviously, he was a sincere religious man.

Why did God bother to put Philip in his path? Because God knew there was more for this hungry soul who was doing all he knew to worship God and learn more about Him. God honored his devoutness by putting a man in his path who could further open his understanding regarding the Scriptures.

"Then Philip opened his mouth, and began at the same scripture, and preached unto him Jesus" (Acts 8:35).

The Bible does not expound on the entire message Philip shared, but what happened next gives evidence as to some of the content.

The horses' ears perked up and their noses quivered. Philip and the Ethiopian looked around. What could be exciting the horses in the middle of a barren desert? A wild animal? No, just up ahead there was a pool of water.

"Hey, do you see what I see?" asked the Ethiopian.

Philip shook his head in amazement, "If you see a pool of water then I think we are seeing the same thing!"

"Ha! What doth hinder me to be baptized?"

"If thou believest with all thine heart, thou mayest," Philip answered.

"I believe that Jesus Christ is the Son of God!" declared the Ethiopian.

After stopping the chariot, both men went down into the water and Philip baptized the sincere man.

As they were coming out of the water, the Ethiopian turned, "Brother Philip, how can I thank—?" "Brother Philip?"

He craned his neck and looked all around. Philip was nowhere to be seen. The Spirit of the Lord had caught him away.

The Bible says "he went on his way rejoicing" (Acts 8:39).

The Ethiopian listened to a man sent from God who opened his understanding regarding the Scriptures. He was immediately obedient and acted upon what God was revealing to him. The result? Joy!

In Acts 10, a devout man that feared God and prayed all of the time, was directed by an angel of God to Peter. Why? Cornelius was obviously religious and sincere. But, when God sees us living for Him as best we know how, He continues to lead us into further revelation. When we hear and obey, He heaps His joy upon us!

Acts 18:24-28 tells of a man named Apollos who was already "mighty in the scriptures" and was an eloquent teacher of the Word. God put a married couple in his path who "expounded unto him the way of God more perfectly" (vs 26). Apollos listened and obeyed and, as a result, God's blessing was upon his ministry.

Perhaps our prayer should be, "Oh God, continue to lead me into further revelation of You and Your Word. Help me to recognize those whom You put in my path to show me Your ways more perfectly. 'Order my steps in thy word' (Psalm 119:133)."

Follow me along a further revelation of the "Roman Road." As we walk along, it is important to know that the epistles (Romans through Jude) are instructional letters written to churches and people who have already had the salvation experience as described repeatedly in the book of Acts. It is in the book of Acts that the church is established and the New Testament way of salvation is revealed. This way of salvation is still the pattern we are to follow today.

"For all have sinned, and come short of the glory of God" (Romans 3:23).

"For the wages of sin is death; but the gift of God is eternal life through Jesus Christ our Lord" (Romans 6:23).

"But God commendeth his love toward us, in that, while we were yet sinners, Christ died for us" (Romans 5:8).

All of us are sinners; therefore, we have the death penalty. But God showed His love for us and took our place through His death on the Cross. Realizing that we have sinned and knowing He has died for our sins, then what do we do? The same question was asked of the apostles after Jesus had risen again in Acts 2:36-38.

"Therefore let all the house of Israel know assuredly, that God hath made that same Jesus, whom ye have crucified, both Lord and Christ.

Now when they heard this, they were pricked in their heart, and said unto Peter and to the rest of the apostles, Men and brethren, what shall we do?

Then Peter said unto them, Repent, and be baptized every one of you in the name of Jesus Christ for the remission of sins, and ye shall receive the gift of the Holy Ghost."

Who gave Peter the authority to answer this all important question? Jesus did in Matthew 16:19.

"And I will give unto thee the keys of the kingdom of heaven: and whatsoever thou shalt bind on earth shall be bound in heaven:

15

and whatsoever thou shalt loose on earth shall be loosed in heaven."

Jesus, Himself, had given instruction as to how to enter the kingdom of heaven in John 3:3-5.

"Jesus answered and said unto him, Verily, verily, I say unto thee, Except a man be born again, he cannot see the kingdom of God.

Nicodemus saith unto him, How can a man be born when he is old? Can he enter the second time into his mother's womb, and be born?

Jesus answered, Verily, verily, I say unto thee, Except a man be born of water and of the Spirit, he cannot enter into the kingdom of God."

Immediately prior to Jesus' ascension, He gave the following instructions in Acts 1:3-5.

"To whom also he shewed himself alive after his passion by many infallible proofs, being seen of them forty days, and speaking of the things pertaining to the kingdom of God:

And, being assembled together with them, commanded them that they should not depart from Jerusalem, but wait for the promise of the Father, which, saith he, ye have heard of me.

For John truly baptized with water, but ye shall be baptized with the Holy Ghost not many days hence."

Note that Jesus said the "promise of the Father" is the "Holy Ghost." Luke also recorded Jesus' instructions prior to His ascension in chapter 24:44-49.

"And he said unto them, These are the words which I spake unto you, while I was yet with you, that all things must be fulfilled, which were written in the law of Moses, and in the prophets, and in the psalms, concerning me.

Then opened he their understanding, that they might understand the scriptures.

And said unto them, Thus it is written, and thus it behoved Christ to suffer, and to rise from the dead the third day:

And that repentance and remission of sins should be preached in his name among all nations, beginning at Jerusalem.

And ye are witnesses of these things.

And, behold, I send the promise of my Father upon you: but tarry ye in the city of Jerusalem, until ye be endued with power from on high."

Obviously, Jesus gave instructions to a group of disciples who believed on Him and that He had died on the Cross. He made sure they completely understood the scriptures. Then, He said that they needed more—repentance, remission of sins (baptism as described in Acts 2:38), and the Holy Ghost.

Don't stop here! Let us continue on to Jerusalem see what happened when they followed Jesus' instructions!

"And when the day of Pentecost was fully come, they were all with one accord in one place.

And suddenly there came a sound from heaven as of a rushing mighty wind, and it filled all the house where they were sitting.

And there appeared unto them cloven tongues like as of fire, and it sat upon each of them.

And they were all filled with the Holy Ghost, and began to speak with other tongues, as the Spirit gave them utterance" (Acts 2:1-4).

What happened? They were filled with the Holy Ghost or Holy Spirit evidenced by speaking in other tongues or languages that they had not learned.

Pentecost is a Jewish feast day that occurs fifty days after the Passover. Many Jews from all over had traveled to Jerusalem for this special day. They heard all these local people speaking in languages native to where they had traveled from. How could this be? They literally asked, "What meaneth this?"

17

"But Peter, standing up with the eleven, lifted up his voice, and said unto them, Ye men of Judaea, and all ye that dwell at Jerusalem, be this known unto you, and hearken to my words:

For these are not drunken, as ye suppose, seeing it is but the third hour of the day.

But this is that which was spoken by the prophet Joel;

And it shall come to pass in the last days, saith God, I will pour out of my Spirit upon all flesh…" (Acts 2:14-17).

Peter, with the support of the eleven apostles, declared that this was the fulfillment of the Old Testament prophecies. This was why Jesus came! Jesus came to provide the way of salvation which is repentance, water baptism in the Name of Jesus, and receiving the Holy Ghost evidenced by speaking in other tongues.

It is important that the evidence of speaking in other tongues when one is filled with the Holy Ghost is not confused with the nine gifts of the Spirit. These nine gifts that are available to the already Spirit-filled believer include divers kinds of tongues and interpretation of tongues (1 Corinthians 12).

One precious lady tried to tell me that tongues had ceased! She opened her Bible to 1 Corinthians 13:8 which says "Charity never faileth: but whether there be prophecies, they shall fail; whether there be tongues, they shall cease; whether there be knowledge, it shall vanish away."

Let us read on in verses 9-10, "For we know in part, and we prophesy in part. But when that which is perfect is come, then that which is in part shall be done away."

There will come a day when perfection comes and the redeemed are gathered in Heaven forever! However, that day has not yet come. Therefore, tongues have not yet ceased. For that matter, neither has prophecy or knowledge.

Let us finish the "Roman Road" with one more scripture.

Romans 14:17 says, "For the kingdom of God is not meat and drink; but righteousness, and peace, and joy in the Holy Ghost." Being born of the Spirit into the kingdom of God brings joy.

If you have yet to be baptized in Jesus' name and receive the infilling of the Holy Ghost evidenced by speaking in other tongues, guess what? There is further revelation for you! When you respond in faith and obedience, God will shower upon you His joy.

The exciting thing about God and His Word is that further revelation never ends! His greatness is unsearchable (Psalm 145:3) and His ways are past finding out (Romans 11:33). The end result of walking in further revelation is always joy!

4. Precedents of Joy

In today's society, instant results are the expectation. Modern conveniences help us wash our clothes and dishes faster, cook our meals quicker, travel faster, and the list goes on. "Snail mail" seems archaic in comparison to e-mail and texting.

Furthermore, debt is sky-rocketing. Who needs to wait, work, and earn what they desire to purchase? Charge it.

Unfortunately, this societal mindset causes people to be undisciplined and unhappy thus leaving them void of joyful living.

Take a moment to reflect. Do you know people who fit this description? Do you fall into this category?

The precious things in life come with a price. They are worth our time, effort, and discipline.

Allow me to share a personal illustration. One Christmas in particular, I invested in a gift for someone and presented it to them. A few months later, I was visiting with them in their home and had to pass through their bedroom. The gift I had bought lay carelessly strewn across the floor along with other various items. In order to reach my destination, I literally had to step over the item. Can you imagine how I felt? This screamed to me that what I had given them with the sacrifice of my own money was of no value or use to them.

How much do you value joy? Do you treasure it? Do you seek to maintain it in your life?

You see, someone has paid a big price for us to obtain true joy. Our Creator robed Himself in flesh, was born of a virgin, lived with His creation, then died in our place on the cross. Why? Hebrews 12:2 says, "Looking unto Jesus the author and finisher of our faith; who for the joy that was set before him endured the cross, despising the shame, and is set down at the right hand of the throne of God."

Jesus endured Calvary so we could walk in relationship with Him, have righteousness, peace, and joy in the Holy Ghost, and live forever with Him in Heaven. He has paid the ultimate price for us to have joy! How do you think He feels when He sees people disregard it?

Furthermore, the God of all glory patiently endured and sacrificed to provide joy to us. How much more should we be willing to do what it takes to have joy ourselves? Is it right for someone to think they can be blatantly disobedient to God and live without spiritual discipline and think they deserve to still have the precious joy our Saviour died for us to have?

Examine yourself. When Jesus looks at me, does He see that I value the joy He has purchased for me? Does He see me living a godly life in obedience to Him and His leadership?

Joy is valuable. Yet, anyone can have it! However, there are things that precede joy. If we truly want joy in our lives, we will discipline ourselves to obtain it.

Repentance is a precedent of joy. One cannot keep sin in their life and expect to have joy also. Repentance is not only telling God you are sorry for your sin, but it is turning away from it and getting it out of your life (2 Corinthians 7:10). Joy and willful sin cannot coexist.

A Biblical example is King David (2 Samuel 11-12). He committed adultery then tried to hide it by having the lady's husband killed in battle. He thought his sin would be hidden and life would go on as usual. But, God loved David enough that He sent Nathan the prophet with a message of chastisement or rebuke for his sin.

"Despise not thou the chastening of the Lord, nor faint when thou art rebuked of him:"

"For whom the Lord loveth he chasteneth" (Hebrews 12:5-6).

"Now no chastening for the present seem to be joyous, but grievous: nevertheless afterward it yieldeth the peaceable fruit of righteousness unto them which are exercised thereby (Hebrews 12:11)."

David responded with immediate contrition. He was quick to repent. His prayer of repentance is recorded in Psalm 51.

"Create in me a clean heart, O God; and renew a right spirit within me."

"Cast me not away from thy presence; and take not thy holy spirit from me."

"Restore unto me the joy of thy salvation; and uphold me with thy free spirit" (Psalm 51:10-12).

When David repented of the sin in his life, His joy was restored! Such is the case with us today.

May I insert here that you will never know the fullness of joy until you have experienced sorrow. An example of this is conviction. In order for David to truly experience joy, the sin in his life had to be addressed. When "Pastor Nathan" brought it to light, David felt sorrow over his sin (conviction). What was his response? Sincere repentance.

Another important precedent to joyful living is a principle that my Pastor and First Lady have frequently taught and preached. A visiting minister, Rev. T.L. Smith, summarized it as "The S.O.C. Principle." Submit. Obey. Commit.

To submit, we must put ourselves under the authority of God and His leadership.

"Submit yourselves therefore to God. Resist the devil, and he will flee from you" (James 4:7).

"Obey them that have the rule over you, and submit yourselves: for they watch for your souls, as they that must give account, that they may do it with joy, and not with grief: for that is unprofitable for you" (Hebrews 13:17).

When you are walking in submission to God and His leadership, you are under the umbrella of God's protection. When you decide to be your own god and lead your own life, you remove yourself from God's protection and blessing and, therefore, all the benefits that come with it—including joy.

Also, notice that in Hebrews 13:17, we are admonished to live in such a way that those God has put in authority in our lives may speak of us joyfully when they give account of us.

The Apostle Paul in his letter to the Philippians said, "For I am in a strait betwixt two, having a desire to depart, and to be with Christ; which is far better:"

"Nevertheless to abide in the flesh is more needful for you."

"And having this confidence, I know that I shall abide and continue with you all for your furtherance and joy of faith;"

"That your rejoicing may be more abundant in Jesus Christ for me by my coming to you again."

We need a pastor in our lives for the "furtherance and joy of faith."

To be truly submissive, you must submit one hundred percent of the time. When those times arise that you are asked to do something that you do not understand or is inconvenient, your true level of submission is tested.

In Deuteronomy 11:26-28, Moses delivered his parting message from God to the children of Israel and it still applies to us today, "Behold, I set before you this day a blessing and a curse;"

"A blessing, if ye obey the commandments of the LORD your God, which I command you this day:"

"And a curse, if ye will not obey the commandments of the LORD your God..."

Obviously, obeying God and His Word are extremely important! If you do not obey, you are cursed. Since that is the case, how can you possess true joy and walk in disobedience to God?

Notice also that Moses was speaking... "A blessing, if ye obey the commandments of the LORD your God, which I command you..." In other words, God told Moses what to say and the people received it from Moses. God used a man to communicate His instructions. The children of Israel then chose if they would obey what Moses said. If they disobeyed what Moses said, they were disobeying what God Himself said.

It is when you are obedient to God's Word and His leadership that you can partake of His blessings and promises.

Hebrews 13:17, as mentioned above, tells us to obey and submit ourselves to God's leadership in our lives.

Lastly but not least in the "S.O.C. Principle" is commitment. My Pastor said, "Commitment means staying loyal to what you said you would do long after the mood you said it in has left you."

What about when it is Sunday morning and you feel exhausted and just want to rest? What about when the church is asking for volunteers for church cleaning or lawn care? What about when the alarm goes off in time for you to have time with God? Are you truly committed?

There is such a lack of commitment in our modern society. Have you ever invited someone for dinner and they did not show up? Have you seen the divorce rates recently? Are we committed to our children? To our church? To our God?

Stay loyal to God! Do not be fickle. Do not let your emotions and circumstances dictate your level of commitment to God. That is not true commitment and it certainly will not produce joy.

Live for God with all your heart, soul, mind, and strength! "There is no very great measure of joy in a half-hearted Christian life. Many so-called Christians have just enough religion to make them miserable. They can no longer enjoy the world and they have not entered into the joy of the Lord." R. A. Torrey (Diamonds for Dusty Roads p. 450).

No matter how you feel, stay loyal to God and to the Truth. Stay loyal to the man of God or pastor in your life. You will find that when feelings fade, joy remains. When your circumstances change, joy remains when you are submitted, obedient, and committed!

Consider Joseph who stayed committed and obedient to God despite being sold into slavery then falsely accused and imprisoned. God honored him, fulfilled his dreams, made him second in command in Egypt, and restored his relationship with his father and family.

This chapter could go on forever but we will end with one more important precedent of joy—prayer.

A life without prayer is a life without joy. If you do not communicate with the Source of joy, how can you have it or maintain it? In His presence is "fullness of joy" (Psalm 16:11).

Psalm 126:5-6 says, "They that sow in tears shall reap in joy."

"He that goeth forth and weepeth, bearing precious seed, shall doubtless come again with rejoicing, bringing his sheaves with him."

When we bring our tears and burdens to God, we will without doubt "reap in joy!"

Personally, spending time in prayer with God has restored my joy more times than I will ever be able to count.

The Bible is full of examples of how prayer changed situations into a joyous outcome.

Because of Daniel's faithful prayer life, he was thrown into the den of lions, however, God honored his commitment to prayer and shut the lions' mouths.

Peter was thrown in prison after Herod had killed James "but prayer was made without ceasing of the church unto God for him" (Acts 12:5). In response to their prayer, God sent an angel to deliver Peter. When he knocked at the gate during the church's prayer meeting, Rhoda heard his voice and "opened not the gate for gladness, but ran in, and told how Peter stood before the gate" (vs. 14).

Note how Daniel could operate in calm joyfulness in his situation because he had a consistent prayer life. In Peter's situation, prayer was made in response to a specific situation. God answered bringing about a joyous result.

Even when life deals us a painful blow, it is our prayer and relationship with God that will sustain us. Do not forget that God said, "When thou passest through the waters, I will be with thee; and through the rivers, they shall not overflow thee: when thou walkest through the fire, thou shalt not be burned; neither shall the flame kindle upon thee" (Isaiah 43:1-2).

More on this subject later.

5. Penny for your thoughts?

What value do you put on thoughts? A penny? A dollar?

Truthfully, our thoughts are more powerful and valuable than we give them credit for.

Have you ever been so caught up in your thoughts that you did not realize what you were doing? I have thrown silverware down the basement stairs, tried to fit the milk jug in the microwave instead of putting it in the refrigerator, put my dinner dishes in the trash instead of the dishwasher, and the list goes on. Obviously, our thoughts can distract us from what we have set out to accomplish.

It is one thing for our thoughts to distract us when completing a routine task. It is quite another when we are being distracted during a spiritual task. Can you focus and absorb God's Word or does your mind wander? What happens when you start to pray?

What do you think? Where does your mind go?

Here is the most important question. With what are you filling your mind?

Throughout my life, I have been an avid reader. If unable to sit and read a book, I will listen to an audio book or the radio while accomplishing routine tasks. My favorite way to relax has been to read clean fiction. Not just any fiction but action packed, dramatic, and suspenseful fiction!

For some reason, I have dreamed the craziest dreams. Easily, my mind can come up with wild scenarios of how something could go wrong. Why? It is what I have put in my mind.

However, as I have followed the leadership of my Pastor and First Lady, there has been a call to "come up higher." Is there anything wrong with a clean action-packed book now and then? Probably not. But how much entertainment are you willing to sacrifice to "walk worthy" and draw nearer to God?

What books do you read? To what do you listen? What music are you putting in your mind? What videos, television shows, and movies are you watching? What internet websites are you frequenting? These are the things with which you are filling your mind.

This is so important! What you put in your mind will impact your thoughts, your dreams, what you say, your actions, and certainly your relationship with God and others.

There is a particular so called Christian author who writes very intense books that are supposed to be spiritual allegories. I was reading all of these books as they came out. Over time, God began to deal with me as these writings began to disturb my spirit. After a while, I quit reading the books altogether. But, the books remained on the shelf in my office.

I began to have very disturbing things happen to me in the night. Soon, I began to see, hear, and feel a dark spirit that would attack me at night. Every time, I would call on the name of Jesus and the attack would stop. I communicated what was happening to my pastor and his wife.

One day, my First Lady told me to put a Bible on my nightstand. I awoke a couple of nights later to see the dark silhouette of a man by my bed, staring at the Bible, and rubbing his hands together in anxiety. I immediately began to speak words in Jesus' name and he disappeared.

When I communicated this to my pastor's wife, she quietly asked, "Are there any books in your house that you feel would cause this?" The name of the so called Christian author immediately came to my mind. What I did not know was God had already revealed this author to her. I went home and threw the books into the trash—the outside trash. After that, the spirits associated with them never disturbed me again.

Working as a nurse in the hospital one night, I had to spend a fair amount of time caring for a sick patient. This patient had the "Sci-Fi" channel on her television all night. I could feel the evil in the atmosphere of her room. The scenes playing were obviously grotesque. I did politely address with her about turning it off. Her response, "It's okay. I know it's not real."

You cannot tell me that what we intake does not matter. As I mature in Christ and as I follow the leadership of the ministry God has put in my life, the things I used to listen to and read have changed.

Proverbs 23:7 says, "For as he thinketh in his heart, so is he."

Americans say, "You are what you eat." Guess what? God says, "You are what you think!"

Examine what you are thinking. Examine what you are putting into your "think tank."

Keep a clean conscience. God gave us our conscience for a reason. Does the book you are reading, what you are watching, or listening to violate your conscience?

2 Corinthians 1:12 says, "For our rejoicing is this, the testimony of our conscience, that in simplicity and godly sincerity, not with fleshly wisdom, but by the grace of God, we have had our conversation in the world…" Wow! We can have joy because we have a clean conscience! Are you living your life before God in simplicity and sincerity?

Cut out distractions! Weed away the weights! We are too close to the rapture to fill our minds with distracting thoughts. We have a race to run!

"Wherefore seeing we also are compassed about with so great a cloud of witnesses, let us lay aside every weight, and the sin which doth so easily beset us, and let us run with patience the race that is set before us" (Hebrews 12:1).

When we align our thoughts with the Word of God, we will have joy! Are you putting joy into your mind? Are you putting godly, uplifting music into your mind?

What are you dwelling upon? Do not even think negatively! Do not think it is safe to let your mind linger on negativity and doubt. Definitely, do not think it is safe to dwell upon sinful things.

If you want joy, peace, righteousness, and the promises of God, think about them!

God is so thorough. He gives us a guideline for our thought life in Philippians 4:8, "Finally, brethren, whatsoever things are true, whatsoever things are honest, whatsoever things are just, whatsoever things are pure, whatsoever things are lovely, whatsoever things are of good report; if there be any virtue, and if there be any praise, think on these things."

The above guideline should serve as a standard for what we read and listen to also.

"Thou wilt keep him in perfect peace, whose mind is stayed on thee: because he trusteth in thee" (Isaiah 26:3).

Consider the great things that God has done for you! (1 Samuel 12:24)

Learn from the Apostle Paul who was falsely accused, imprisoned, and put on trial. In the middle of his seemingly negative circumstance, he stood and said, "I think myself happy" (Acts 26:2).

What about David? In 1 Samuel 30, the Bible says he was "greatly distressed." His family and all he owned had been stolen from him. The city he lived in had been burned with fire. That sounds distressing to me! We all have our distressing tales to tell. We are not in heaven yet.

Not only had David lost all he owned, but his own people wanted to stone him to death. Yet, "David encouraged himself in the LORD his God" (1 Samuel 30:6). Then, he got with the man of God and prayed. God gave him a directive. David acted upon it and "David recovered all" (1 Samuel 30:18).

Instead of dwelling on how negative his situation was, David encouraged himself in the Lord.

Do you want joy in the midst of your life? Think joy! Think about God. Think encouraging thoughts. Your thoughts will impact how you speak and how you act.

Remember, do not go by your feelings. Feelings are fickle. They change with the wind.

When negative thoughts enter your mind (because they will), do not let them stay there. Choose not to dwell on them.

I have played the piano in my church for many years. Countless times while playing during the service, thoughts have popped into my mind, "You're just playing this good to show off because there's a visiting minister here." "You can't worship like you want because you have to play this piano." "You're a prideful musician." In the past, I would think these thoughts, claim them as my own, and then feel guilty. Finally, I realized that when they come, let them pass right on through. Instead, keep playing with whatever measure of skill God has blessed me with and continue to focus on worshipping Him.

Similarly, whatever the source of thoughts that bring condemnation, pride, guilt, and potential damage to your relationship with God, choose not to dwell on them. Let them pass and begin to think on Jesus.

Cover your mind with the "helmet of salvation" (Ephesians 6:17). Plead the blood of Jesus over your mind.

"Jesus, align our thought lives with how You would have us to think!"

6. What are you calling forth?

The temple filled with the scent of incense. Zacharias savored the smell as he raised his hands in worship to God. The Lord had been good to him and his wife, Elisabeth. They had served Him together throughout the past many years. Yes, they were old — very old. His main desire for which he and Elisabeth had often prayed was for a child. But, year after year had passed until now; well, he no longer hoped. It was too late. He and Elisabeth were considered elderly citizens.

He sighed then resumed his custom of offering the incense for the children of Israel. He could hear their voices blending in prayer outside the temple door.

What was that noise? He sensed that someone was there. How could they have come in? He had not heard the door open.

Zacharias opened his eyes and looked around. Then he gasped! On the right side of the altar of incense stood a man! Not just any man — he was an angel of the Lord.

Unable to help himself, he shook in fear as he stared at the angel. He looked the angel over hoping this was not judgment for being late for work two days ago. He looked into his eyes. They looked kind.

Then the angel spoke, "Fear not, Zacharias: for thy prayer is heard; and thy wife Elisabeth shall bear thee a son, and thou shalt call his name John."

"And thou shalt have joy and gladness; and many shall rejoice at his birth."

Zacharias' mouth hung open in disbelief. Really? After all these years? You have got to be kidding me!

The angel continued to speak of how his son would be filled with the Holy Ghost from the womb and turn many children of Israel to God. His son would literally prepare the way for the coming Messiah. Seriously? It had been four hundred years since they had heard a single prophecy!

Finally, the angel stopped speaking and calmly looked into Zacharias' eyes.

Zacharias looked skeptical and responded, "Whereby shall I know this? For I am an old man, and my wife well stricken in years."

The angel spoke again, "I am Gabriel, that stand in the presence of God; and am sent to speak unto thee, and to shew thee these glad tidings."

If God literally sent an angel to speak to you and you still doubted, what would it take for you to believe? Hello?

The angel continued, "And, behold, thou shalt be dumb, and not able to speak, until the day that these things shall be performed, because thou believest not my words, which shall be fulfilled in their season."

Perhaps Zacharias opened his mouth to say, "Wait! I take my words of unbelief back!" But if he did, nothing came out of his mouth. The angel disappeared leaving him standing there alone and unable to voice any more words of doubt so the promise of God could be fulfilled.

Approximately six months later, God sent Gabriel to Elisabeth's cousin, Mary. Mary was a virgin who was engaged to Joseph.

Perhaps she was making her wedding dress or making other wedding plans. The Bible does not specify. But, whatever she was doing was interrupted by Gabriel.

"Hail, thou that art highly favoured, the Lord is with thee: blessed art thou among women."

Maybe Mary thought, "Are you talking to me?" Then, there was no one else in the room but her. She peered at the angel fearfully. She had never seen one before.

The angel continued, "Fear not, Mary: for thou hast found favour with God."

"And, behold, thou shalt conceive in thy womb, and bring forth a son, and shalt call his name Jesus."

"He shall be great, and shall be called the Son of the Highest: and the Lord God shall give unto him the throne of his father David:"

"And he shall reign over the house of Jacob for ever; and of his kingdom there shall be no end."

Mary was stunned. She was the one chosen to give birth to the Messiah? Carefully, she asked, "How shall this be, seeing I know not a man?"

A valid question.

The angel responded, "The Holy Ghost shall come upon thee, and the power of the Highest shall overshadow thee: therefore also that holy thing which shall be born of thee shall be called the Son of God."

Wow! Mary listened as the angel spoke that her elderly cousin, Elisabeth, was six months pregnant and that nothing was impossible with God. Her response, "Behold the handmaid of the Lord; be it unto me according to thy word."

Note the difference between her response and the response of Zacharias. One voiced disbelief while the other said, "Be it unto me according to thy word." Mary chose to verify the promise with the words of her mouth.

Both accounts are in Luke 1.

What are you calling forth? Are you verifying the words of God with your speech or voicing doubt? Fortunately, God does not strike us dumb when we voice doubt because if He did, many of us would have chronic laryngitis!

Which would you prefer? Inability to speak doubt and the promises of God fulfilled or voicing doubt and the promises of God not being fulfilled?

You see, there is creative power in our words. In the beginning, God spoke and it was created. Then, He breathed into the first human His breath of life. Whatever God says, it happens! His creative power flows through us. Oh, be careful little mouth what you say!

There is a reason for this chapter to follow the previous chapter. Jesus said in Matthew 12:34, "For out of the abundance of the heart the mouth speaketh." What you have been harboring in your heart and thinking about will come out of your mouth. Your thought life will naturally spill over into the words you say. Do not entertain doubtful thoughts!

In reference to Abraham being the father of many nations, Romans 4:17 tells us that God "calleth those things which be not as though they were." Abraham is the father of many nations. We know this to be an historical fact now. However, God called it forth before the natural eyes could see it.

God's creative power of speech is in us.

Think about the words you have spoken recently. What are you saying will happen? How are you describing your life and situations?

I had a co-worker who always spoke so negatively about her health. When she had a headache, she literally said she must have a brain tumor. With every ailment she suffered, she spoke of a major problem being present in her body.

I had prayed with her several times. I told her multiple times when she would speak negatively about herself, "Don't say that!" What happened? I watched her get sicker and sicker until she finally had to quit because of all her health issues.

Are you not seeing God's promises fulfilled? Think about what you are saying. Are you voicing words of unbelief or are you speaking the promises into existence?

What are you creating with your words? Maybe you are reading this and thinking, "But, my circumstances really are terrible! I'm just speaking the truth!" Quit creating more negativity and start changing your circumstances with your speech! However, be sure your speech is lining up with the Word of God and His will.

Proverbs 18:20-21 says, "A man's belly shall be satisfied with the fruit of his mouth; and with the increase of his lips shall he be filled."

"Death and life are in the power of the tongue: and they that love it shall eat the fruit thereof."

Furthermore, Ecclesiastes 5:2-3 says, "Be not rash with thy mouth, and let not thine heart be hasty to utter any thing before God: for God is in heaven, and thou upon earth: therefore let thy words be few."

"For a dream cometh through the multitude of business; and a fool's voice is known by multitude of words."

Our prayer should be, "Set a watch, O LORD, before my mouth; keep the door of my lips" (Psalm 141:3).

But what if you are just "venting?" What if you are pouring out your frustrations before God? Is that okay?

Personally, when I have been upset about situations and complained to God, I have felt worse rather than better.

There is a difference between bringing your problems to God in humble faith believing He knows what is best and is able to work the miraculous and coming before Him in anger, doubt, and with a complaining attitude! Note also that the verse above, Ecclesiastes 5:2 says, "Be not rash with thy mouth, and let not thine heart be hasty to utter any thing before God..."

Proverbs 29:11 says, "A fool uttereth all his mind."

Be careful and respectful when you come before the Lord God.

If you want to know how God feels about complaining, read about the Israelites in the Old Testament. They complained a lot! The overall outcome was never joyous.

Psalm 106:25 says the Israelites "murmured in their tents." What are you saying in the privacy of your home? It is never permissive to speak negativity. And know that if you speak the negative, you are speaking it into existence.

Regardless of how you feel or what you see or how long you have waited, speak positive! Speak the promises of God! Speak healing! Speak salvation! Speak provision! Speak joy!

Determine to be intentional about what you speak. "I am purposed that my mouth shall not transgress" (Psalm 17:3).

"Moving his lips he bringeth evil to pass" (Proverbs 16:30).

Conversely, "A man hath joy by the answer of his mouth: and a word spoken in due season, how good is it!" (Proverbs 15:23)

Instead of worrying and voicing doubt, trust God. "Whoso trusteth in the LORD, happy is he" (Proverbs 16:20).

My pastor recently said, "It's easier to grovel than to grow. God wants us to grow."

Do you want to grow? Do you want joy? Get a hold of what God is saying to you today and your life will be changed.

7. Joy Thieves

Jesus told His disciples, "...your joy no man taketh from you" (John 16:22).

No one can steal our joy! Then how do we lose it? Where does it go?

No man can take our joy but there are things that seek to steal it from us. I will call them "joy thieves."

The devil does not want God's people to have joy, because he knows just how powerful a joy-filled child of God is. If he can cause us to lose our joy, he can steal our faith, peace, praise, and much more. Joy is a precious treasure. We must learn to guard against the joy thieves.

Honestly, the list of joy thieves is quite long. We will look at just a few of them in this book.

Daniel 7:25 speaks of the enemy seeking to "wear out the saints of the most High." Weariness can be a joy thief.

Have you ever been so exhausted that you did not want to do anything? Perhaps you just wanted to go to bed or be at home. You try to function and it is like the wheels of your mind are turning slowly through a dense fog.

Sometimes, this happens because your body is letting you know, "Hey! Stop! I need a break. I need some rest!" In those times, we need to arrange our schedule to respond with rest.

Other times, it is an attack of the enemy using weariness. Do not let the enemy slow you down and steal your joy with weariness. There are times we must push through weariness. Never let weariness stop your church attendance, prayer time, time in God's Word, etc. These are sources of joy! Faithfulness to God will maintain your joy.

God does gives us a promise to stand upon in these times. "He giveth power to the faint; and to them that have no might he increaseth strength."

"Even the youths shall faint and be weary, and the young men shall utterly fall:"

"But they that wait upon the LORD shall renew their strength; they shall mount up with wings as eagles; they shall run, and not be weary; and they shall walk, and not faint" (Isaiah 40:29-31).

Another joy thief is lack of submission.

It is so important for us to keep our minds saturated with the Word of God, to pray, to be in God's house, and spend time with our Heavenly Father. When we do not, it is so easy for the enemy to slip thoughts into our minds that seem to be true but are really twisted lies. When we dwell on these thoughts, it begins to show in our words and actions as an unsubmissive, rebellious spirit. Get this – an unsubmissive spirit makes you very gullible!

Our world today says you do not need a spiritual authority in your life. But the truth is you need a pastor—not just any pastor, but the one God has put in your life.

"And I will give you pastors according to mine heart, which shall feed you with knowledge and understanding" (Jeremiah 3:15).

"And he gave some, apostles; and some, prophets; and some, evangelists; and some, pastors and teachers;"

"For the perfecting of the saints, for the work of the ministry, for the edifying of the body of Christ:"

"Till we all come in the unity of the faith, and of the knowledge of the Son of God, unto a perfect man, unto the measure of the stature of the fulness of Christ:"

"That we be no more children, tossed to and fro, and carried about with every wind of doctrine, by the sleight of men, and cunning craftiness, whereby they lie in wait to deceive;"

"But speaking the truth in love, may grow up into him in all things, which is the head, even Christ" (Ephesians 4:11-15).

Submission is one of the precedents of joy. To have joy, we must be submissive to God and His authority in our lives. We must be obedient with a right attitude in the big things and small things.

As we discovered in chapter 4, being rebellious and unsubmissive is not a picture of joy, but it stinks in the nostrils of God! It brings misery.

One notable example of someone who had an unsubmissive spirit to God and the man of God was Jezebel. In her day, the man of God was Elijah. Her husband was King Ahab. You can read the end result of her rebellious life in 2 Kings 9:30-37.

To be submissive is not a weakness, but a great strength. It ushers God's blessing, favor, and protection into your life.

Watch out for this joy thief! Stay submissive.

The third joy thief comes in the disguise of inflexibility. Uh oh! If you have yet to discover that things do not always go as planned, then you must have been born yesterday.

If a change of plans or delay upsets you and displaces your joy, you need to ask God to help you be flexible.

One evening from out of nowhere, I got this craving for a burger from McDonald's. This is odd for me because I generally prefer other restaurants. But, I found myself sitting in the drive through line at McDonald's. I could not figure out what burger I wanted. Finally, I realized that I had been sitting there for several minutes. I peered at the vehicle ahead of me. The driver had opened their door and was sitting there staring at the menu with their finger in their mouth – literally. This continued for several more minutes.

Frustration began to build. Why didn't they just go inside? Finally, I pulled out of the line and went inside myself. I felt upset inwardly but put on a big smile for the cashier. I explained that I was in the mood for a burger but I could not figure out which one.

The cashier said, "What kind of burger are you craving?"

"I would like a spicy one with some crunch."

"You should get the jalapeno crunch burger then!"

I thanked him for recommending an awesome burger. Then, feeling a nudge of the Holy Ghost, I pulled out a church invitation and told him that since he had helped me discover an awesome burger, I would like to recommend to him an awesome church!

His response, "Thank you, ma'am. I'll surely come."

I left knowing there was a reason I had been delayed in the line and ended up going inside. God wanted to put me in the path of a hungry soul.

We may not always understand the reason for changes in plans or delays. However, when we are secure in our daily walk with God, we know that He directs our steps. If He wanted things to go as we planned, they would happen that way.

The key? Learn to be flexible.

Joseph's life was not going as he planned. But, he was flexible! He did not let go of his joy but made the best of every situation. What happened? God's promises came true in ways he probably never thought would happen.

How inconvenient was it for Mary when she became pregnant? She was engaged. Her fiancé did not believe her and was going to quietly break it off. She even fled to her cousin, Elisabeth, for a few months. However, she was flexible and God came through for her.

Another wicked, sly joy thief is unforgiveness. How can you possess joy and harbor unforgiveness in your heart? Unforgiveness breeds bitterness. Bitterness and joy cannot abide in the same location. They are two totally different "fruits."

Jesus said in Matthew 7:16, "Ye shall know them by their fruits."

He continued, "Even so every good tree bringeth forth good fruit; but a corrupt tree bringeth forth evil fruit."

"A good tree cannot bring forth evil fruit, neither can a corrupt tree bring forth good fruit."

"Every tree that bringeth not forth good fruit is hewn down, and cast into the fire."

"Wherefore by their fruits ye shall know them" (vs 17-20).

Joy is a fruit of the Spirit. Unforgiveness and bitterness are evil fruits.

The Apostle Paul wrote to the Ephesians to put away bitterness and to forgive one another.

"Let all bitterness, and wrath, and anger, and clamour, and evil speaking, be put away from you, with all malice:"

"And be ye kind one to another, tenderhearted, forgiving one another, even as God for Christ's sake hath forgiven you" (Ephesians 4:31-32).

Jesus said in Matthew 6:12, 14-15, "And forgive us our debts, as we forgive our debtors."

"For if ye forgive men their trespasses, your heavenly Father will also forgive you."

"But if ye forgive not men their trespasses, neither will your Father forgive your trespasses."

We are to forgive others the same way that Jesus forgives us. Notice that Jesus sees how we forgive others. If we are not forgiving those who have wronged us, He withholds His forgiveness from us.

Furthermore, He instructs us in Matthew 11:25-26, "And when ye stand praying, forgive, if ye have ought against any that your Father also which is in heaven may forgive you your trespasses."

"But if ye do not forgive, neither will your Father which is in heaven forgive your trespasses."

Truthfully, God directly moved on me to include unforgiveness specifically as a joy thief in this book. When you harbor unforgiveness, you are hurting yourself! Plus, you are permitting the loss of your joy.

In his book "Better Than Medicine: A Merry Heart," Leroy Brownlow said, "Forgiveness is both a tranquilizer and a stimulant; a tranquilizer which settles nerves and a stimulant which invigorates health" (pg 96).

Take care of wrongs as they happen. Forgive immediately! Do not let unforgiveness in for one minute. Forgive yourself as well as others. Do not hold a grudge against God either.

Rev. Vickie Vernon says, "You become what you don't forgive."

What a powerful and true statement!

She has also said, "Shame is a grudge you hold against others, yourself, and God. Once the layers come off, we're whole," and she added "Bind the voice of the accuser of the brethren. The devil accuses us of what he is."

Forgiveness is a beautiful thing. Forgiveness brings joy.

Jesus died to bring us forgiveness of sins and redemption even though we certainly did not deserve it. Shouldn't we let His character and mission continue in us?

Another joy thief is pride.

A prime example of this is found in Isaiah 16:6-14. Let us examine the following verses.

"We have heard of the pride of Moab; he is very proud: even of his haughtiness, and his pride, and his wrath..." (vs 6).

"I will water thee with my tears... for the shouting for thy summer fruits and for thy harvest is fallen. And gladness is taken away, and joy out of the plentiful field; and in the vineyards there shall be no singing, neither shall there be shouting..." (vs 9-10).

Remember, "Pride goeth before destruction, and an haughty spirit before a fall. Better it is to be of an humble spirit with the lowly, than to divide the spoil with the proud" (Proverbs 16:18-19).

It does not take a rocket scientist to realize that being prideful robs you of joy.

Think on this, "A man's pride shall bring him low: but honour shall uphold the humble in spirit" (Proverbs 29:23).

Also, consider 1 Peter 5:5-6, "Likewise, ye younger, submit yourselves unto the elder. Yea, all of you be subject one to another, and be clothed with humility: for God resisteth the proud, and giveth grace to the humble."

"Humble yourselves therefore under the mighty hand of God, that he may exalt you in due time."

Pride equals destruction. Humility equals God's grace, favor, and exaltation.

Therefore, guard against the joy thief of pride. Embrace humility and God will maintain your joy.

Lastly, a joy thief out to get you is worry. Basically, worry is lack of faith in God.

Seriously, He has everything under control. If we are walking in relationship with Him and submitted to Him, what do we have to worry about? He literally takes care of our every need.

In a personal time of prayer one day, I was asking God about some personal financial needs. I began to pray in the Spirit. Suddenly, a Scripture in English began to come out my mouth. It was the familiar passage of Matthew 6:33, "But seek ye first the kingdom of God, and his righteousness; and all these things shall be added unto you."

I felt impressed to look it up and started reading a few verses prior... "Therefore take no thought, saying, What shall we eat? or, What shall we drink? or, Wherewithal shall we be clothed?"

"(For after all these things do the Gentiles seek:) for your heavenly Father knoweth that ye have need of all these things" (Matthew 6:31-32).

Our Heavenly Father knows our needs. When we are putting Him first, we do not need to worry.

Instead, He gives us peace that passes all understanding (Philippians 4:7). He tells us to trust in Him with all of our hearts and not to lean on our own understanding (Proverbs 3:5).

It is impossible to worry when we are trusting God and filled with His peace. Do not let worry steal your joy! Have faith in God (Mark 11:22).

To guard our joy is not always easy. Sometimes, it seems easier to give in to the bombardment of the above joy thieves. It takes personal discipline and determination. We must discipline ourselves to be faithful in prayer, the Word of God, and the house of God. We must discipline ourselves to push through weariness, be submissive, flexible, forgiving, and humble.

You will discover that the more time you spend in relationship with God, the harder it is for these joy thieves to be successful.

8. Joy In the Journey

"Ruth, dear, I've been thinking."

"Yes, Naomi?"

"You know that ruggedly handsome gentleman who has been so generous and kind to you?"

"You mean Boaz?"

"Of course, dear. Did you know that he is a close kin to us?"

"I didn't know."

"Tonight, he will be at the threshingfloor removing chaff from the barley. So, go wash up, put on your most fragrant perfume, and…you know…look cute!"

"Excuse me, Mother?"

"You heard me. Watch him but don't let yourself be seen by anyone. Then, when he lies down, go and uncover his feet and lay down."

"You had me until you said feet."

"Seriously, my daughter!"

"Yes ma'am."

Truthfully, the above dialogue is not an exact quote of Ruth 3:1-5. However, I am sure that it was not an expressionless and dull conversation either! Do you hear the love in Naomi's voice for her daughter-in-law? Or, can you imagine the excitement and hope swelling in Ruth as she responded in obedience to her mother-in-law?

Joy was present as Ruth tip-toed down to the threshingfloor that night and was soon discovered by her husband-to-be, Boaz.

Remember when we referenced Peter earlier showing up at the gate in Acts 12?

Knock! Knock!

Peter looked around the dark streets. Since an angel had just led him past two bands of soldiers and straight through an iron gate, he knew he had nothing to fear. He was free! He was alive! Now, if only he could let the praying saints inside the house know! Their prayers were answered!

He listened as their fervent pleas to God on his behalf reached his ears and wanted to shout, "I'm here! I am right out here!"

Inside the house, Rhoda had been praying but had paused. What was that sound? Was someone knocking at the gate? But, who would be knocking at this hour? She proceeded to pray.

There it was again! She was sure she heard someone knocking. Or was it her imagination?

"I'll go investigate myself. It would be rude to disrupt a prayer meeting over nothing."

Silently, she made her way to the gate.

Knock! Knock!

She gasped! Then, she let out a timid, "Hello?"

"Rhoda? Is that you? This is Peter. Would you let me in?"

Now she gasped in delight! Peter! The very one they had been praying for without ceasing was literally standing at the gate! That was his voice beyond all doubt!

She was so ecstatic with joy that she forgot to let the beloved apostle in and ran back to the praying saints.

"Hey! Excuse me!"

A few heads raised and sent her some looks that said, "Don't disturb our prayer." Then, they reverently lowered again.

She jumped up and down for joy. More heads came up and more looks came her way.

"Listen! Peter is at the gate! Peter is at the gate!"

One lady said, "Poor Rhoda. She's gone loopy on us."

"I always thought she was a little...you know...touched in the head."

"Land o' Goshen! Let me feel your forehead, child! You must have a fever."

Rhoda pleaded now, "Seriously! Peter is at the gate. I heard his voice!"

"Ha! The voice of his angel. They done killed 'im!"

Rhoda shook her head, "Go see for yourself!"

Knock! Knock!

Everyone in the house went silent.

"His angel's at the gate," one aged man shook his head sadly.

The owner of the house, Mary, rose up and said, "We might as well open the gate."

The band of prayer warriors hesitantly opened the gate... and gaped in astonishment! The answer to their prayers stood before them.

Perhaps they laughed at themselves for thinking it was his angel and for thinking that Rhoda had gone mad. What joy must have filled their hearts as their beloved leader stood before them alive and well!

Learn to laugh. Learn to enjoy the journey!

In Deuteronomy 28, many curses were listed "Because thou servedst not the LORD thy God with joyfulness, and with gladness of heart, for the abundance of all things" (verse 47). Conversely, we are blessed if we serve the LORD our God with joyfulness and gladness of heart for the abundance of all things!

Psalm 100:2 says "Serve the LORD with gladness."

Do not sweat the small stuff. Learn to laugh! Look for ways to create joy in the journey.

One Sunday morning during Sunday School, all the classes combined in the sanctuary for a special presentation. After a quick trip to the restroom, I joined them.

Since I am on the scrapbook committee, I began to position myself at key moments to get good pictures – often at the front of the whole church. As soon as the classes were dismissed, a first time guest came up to me and let me know that I had tucked the back hem of my skirt in my undergarments.

I had two options. I could practically die with embarrassment and mourn the rest of the day or fix it quick and laugh. I chose the latter.

Do not turn everything into a crisis. Learn to laugh and move on!

One time I was sharing a hotel room with another lady in the church during a conference. She often experienced back pain and brought remedies for relief with her.

Focused on being ready on time, I stopped at the sink, grabbed my toothbrush, quickly applied toothpaste, and began brushing my teeth. After a few moments I thought, "This tastes weird."

I took another close look at the "toothpaste." It was my roommate's muscle relaxer!

Quickly, I began to rinse my mouth as thoroughly as possible then tested my voice to be sure the medicated cream had not had time to work! I still laugh about this today.

One night I was exhausted and it was time to go to bed. However, I kept hearing the sound of revving engines. They were so loud! How could I possibly rest with that going on? I lived relatively close to the busiest street in town. Figuring that had to be where the commotion was coming from, I pointed in the direction of the noise and commanded, "In the name of Jesus you will stop!"

After a few minutes, it stopped. I went to sleep.

The next morning at work, one of my co-workers complained to me, "I drove an hour to your town for the annual tractor pulls.

They usually last past midnight but last night it was over by ten o'clock!"

She was so disappointed. I just looked at her trying to put on my sympathetic face and not break out into laughter in front of her.

Are you wishing we were in a conversation and not a book? I am sure you have some stories to tell also. If not, create some! Look for them! There is joy in your journey! There are reasons to laugh!

Have you ever received one of those "IRS" phone calls saying you must pay immediately or you will be arrested? The first time I received such a call, I had not been forewarned. I listened with growing concern as the voice on the other line told me that if I did not pay immediately, the police would show up in forty-five minutes and arrest me. I would go to jail. Unsure if I was making a right decision or not and sending up silent prayers, I refused to pay and hung up.

I sat at my kitchen table alone and visibly shaking. What would I do? What would the church and community think when I got arrested? What would happen to my witness? I called the First Lady of my church who assured me that it was a scam. No, the police were not coming to arrest me. Although I believed her, I still peaked out my windows for the next hour.

Our church was having a children's revival with a guest children's evangelist. Immediately prior to the service, I discovered we were out of toilet paper in the downstairs bathrooms. I grabbed a roll of toilet paper and started down the stairs. I heard footsteps coming at the bottom of the stairs from around the corner. Figuring it was one of the gentlemen in my church, I threw the toilet paper at him as he came around the bend and yelled, "Think fast!"

I met the surprised gaze of the guest evangelist. He passed the toilet paper back and suppressed a grin as I profusely apologized.

Again, learn to laugh. "I will rejoice in the LORD, I will joy in the God of my salvation" (Habakkuk 3:18).

We go through good times and bad times. There are ups and downs in the journey of life. As children of the King, we can walk in assurance knowing that He works all things together for our good (Romans 8:28).

Here is another way to think.

Zephaniah 3:17 says, "The LORD thy God in the midst of thee is mighty; he will save, he will rejoice over thee with joy; he will rest in his love, he will joy over thee with singing."

Wow! God is rejoicing and joying and singing over me? Yes!

Question... If I examine my current attitude about my circumstances and life in general, am I making it easy for my Creator to sing and rejoice over me? Can He sing and rejoice over a complaining and "woe is me" attitude?

I took my niece and nephew grocery shopping with me. Before getting out of the vehicle, I instructed them that I would not be buying them a toy this time but they could help me put food items in the cart.

The moment we walked in the door, my nephew pointed at a $0.99 hot car he wanted. I reminded him of what had been said in the vehicle. He pouted and cried. After a few minutes, I looked around and he had sneaked out of my sight. Momentarily, he appeared with a grin holding the hot car with a receipt! He had scrounged around and found some quarters in the store. Then, he went through the checkout himself and a "kind" patron behind him had made up the difference and helped him buy the car.

What did I do? I took it from him.

Did I want him to have that toy? Yes. Did I want him to be happy? Yes. However, his attitude got in the way. Instead of trusting that I had his best interest in mind, he took things into his own hands to try to create a joyous outcome for himself. Instead, he ruined it.

I had planned to buy it later and surprise him. Now, I could not. His attitude and actions prevented me.

Do we do that to God sometimes? Do we look at our situations through our natural eyes and have a wrong attitude and take things into our own hands? Do we want something badly and it seems that God will not give it to us? Or, He does not work things out the way we want?

On every account our Heavenly Father is looking at us in love wanting the best for us. But, if we do not choose joy and trust in Him, we tie His hands. We could literally prevent His blessings from flowing in our lives.

We are children of God. He offers us joy and so much more. A parent wants to give their child the best but gives them boundaries for safety. If a parent lets a child do whatever they want however they want whenever they want and everything they want, they will be spoiled.

What is the disposition of a spoiled child? It is not pleasant. They pout and throw fits very easily. Their happiness over what they want is short then they want something else and become moody and angry when it does not happen immediately. This is definitely not a joyful child.

There are precedents to joy just like there are precedents to the privileges in a child's life. We are children of the best Parent ever – we are children of King Jesus. He is our Heavenly Father.

No matter what life looks like, if you are in relationship with Jesus, you can choose joy. Choosing joy will cause your Heavenly Father to want to bless you more!

God Himself is the source of joy—not His way of working. We do not understand Him. His ways are higher than our ways (Isaiah 55:8-13). What He has said will happen. His word will not return void. It will prosper. But, it takes time just like it takes time from the planting of a seed to the harvesting of the fruit it produces. If we are patient and trust in Him, we will "go out with joy, and be led forth with peace" and experience the blessings of God which are always so much better than what we originally imagined. Thank God that things do not always go the way we want but the way He wants.

Colossians 1:10-11 says, "That ye might walk worthy of the Lord unto all pleasing, being fruitful in every good work, and increasing in the knowledge of God;"

"Strengthened with all might, according to his glorious power, unto all patience and longsuffering with joyfulness..."

You mean to say we can have joy as we are patient and longsuffering in this life? Yes.

Please take careful thought of what is being written here.

The latter part of Romans 4 tells of Abraham who "staggered not at the promise of God through unbelief; but was strong in faith, giving glory to God; And being fully persuaded, that what he had promised, he was able also to perform" (Romans 4:20-21).

Abraham received a promise from God that he would be the father of many nations. Yet, he did not see fulfillment of the promised son until he was one hundred years old and his wife ninety years old! He had to endure through times that he did not understand God's way of working.

Straight from this context is Romans 5:1, "Therefore being justified by faith, we have peace with God through our Lord Jesus Christ."

Stop and think for a minute on the phrase "peace with God." Are you at peace with God? When tragedy strikes your life, are you at peace with God? When things do not happen when you thought they would happen, are you at peace with God?

Do not get mad at God. It is a carnal tendency to become bitter against Him and ask, "God, how could You let this happen?" "Why are You doing this to me?"

We must learn to submit to Him and trust Him and not lean on our own understanding (Proverbs 3:5). Learn to be at peace with God. This will bring joy. To be offended in Him will rob you of joy.

Romans 5 continues, "By whom also we have access by faith into this grace wherein we stand, and rejoice in hope of the glory of God. And not only so, but we glory in tribulations also; knowing that tribulation worketh patience; And patience, experience; and experience, hope: And hope maketh not ashamed; because the love of God is shed abroad in our hearts by the Holy Ghost which is given unto us" (vs 2-5).

Let God work in you and you will not be ashamed.

What is another way to create joy in the journey? Make your world a better place.

Many years ago, Rev. Kenneth Pate taught a Bible lesson on "Making Your World a Better Place." Are you creating joy for others? Do it! It is fun!

You be the one to make a phone call to a lonely friend. Drop a card in the mail to brighten someone's day. Send an "I'm thinking of you" text. Remember your friends' birthdays.

Be thoughtful! Be kind. Make the world a better place for your children, your spouse, your Pastor and First Lady, your church family, your neighbors, your co-workers, etc.

Not only will you bring joy to their lives, but you will find it creates joy in your life also.

Leroy Brownlow said, "Happiness, like a tide that flows in and out, will come back to you after you have sent it to others" (Better Than Medicine: A Merry Heart, pg 104).

See? There are countless ways to find joy in your journey. Look for it! Create it! Make it happen for others! But always remember, keep walking in relationship with your Heavenly Father who is rejoicing over you.

9. Joy from Relationship with the Father

"And in that day thou shalt say, O LORD, I will praise thee: though thou wast angry with me, thine anger is turned away, and thou comfortedst me.

Behold, God is my salvation; I will trust, and not be afraid: for the LORD JEHOVAH is my strength and my song; he also is become my salvation.

Therefore with joy shall ye draw water out of the wells of salvation.

And in that day shall ye say, Praise the LORD, call upon his name, declare his doings among the people, make mention that his name is exalted.

Sing unto the LORD; for he hath done excellent things: this is known in all the earth.

Cry out and shout, thou inhabitant of Zion: for great is the Holy One of Israel in the midst of thee" (Isaiah 12).

Who is our source of joy? Jesus. He is our strength and song. We can joyfully draw from the wells of our relationship with Jesus!

The Hebrew word for "salvation" as used in Isaiah 12 is "Yeshuw'ah." Sound familiar? Yeshuw'ah is a Hebrew name for JEHOVAH! The name Jesus means that JEHOVAH has become our salvation.

Yeshuw'ah literally means deliverance, aid, victory, prosperity, health, help, and welfare (Holmann's Bible Dictionary). There is a bountiful supply of all we need in Jesus.

No matter how badly the storms of life are buffeting you, you can ride them out peacefully and with joy when you are walking in relationship with the Father.

Jesus is the Father (Isaiah 9:6, John 10:30, John 14:8-11). He is the Father in Creation (Malachi 2:10, Colossians 1:15-17). The name of the Father is Jesus (John 5:43).

Jesus is our heavenly Father.

In the chapter on "Joy Thieves," remember when I was praying over financial needs? I was just spending time with my Heavenly Father and bringing the concern to Him.

My Father's answer to my concerns? "Don't worry about it. I know you need these things. Put Me first and I'll take care of it" (Matthew 6:31-33).

In this same chapter of Matthew we discover more about how to interact with our Heavenly Father. Matthew 6:6, "But thou, when thou prayest, enter into thy closet, and when thou hast shut thy door, pray to thy Father which is in secret, and thy Father which seeth in secret shall reward thee openly."

This verse alone should alert us to the extreme importance and vitality of maintaining a personal prayer life. Pray to Him when you are in need. Pray to Him when you do not have a care in the world. Pray to Him daily. That is true relationship which will sustain you and keep your joy tank full.

Doesn't a healthy marriage require daily communication? How long would a marriage last if the couple only interacted when one needed something from the other?

The same is true of our Heavenly Father. He is so patient with us. He desires to be not only our Maker and Savior, but the Lover of our soul with whom we daily communicate.

Here is a suggestion. Every day, give Him a smile. That is right! Look upward and give your Father a big smile! Good morning, Jesus.

What a nugget of treasure Matthew 6 is! Why? Jesus also gave us "The Lord's Prayer" in verses 9-13.

"Our Father which art in heaven, Hallowed be thy name.

Thy kingdom come. Thy will be done in earth, as it is in heaven.

Give us this day our daily bread.

And forgive us our debts, as we forgive our debtors.

And lead us not into temptation, but deliver us from evil: For thine is the kingdom, and the power, and the glory, for ever. Amen."

Jesus gave us a pattern of prayer. It begins with coming before Him as our Heavenly Father.

When we approach Him, we must understand not only that He is our Heavenly Father, but also that we are His children.

Am I a child of God? Romans 8:9 says, "But ye are not in the flesh, but in the Spirit, if so be that the Spirit of God dwell in you. Now if any man have not the Spirit of Christ, he is none of his." Have you been filled with the Holy Spirit?

Have you taken on the family name in baptism? (Acts 2:38, Acts 4:12, Acts 8:12, Acts 10:48, Acts 19:5)

When we approach our Father, we are not beggars. We do not have to whine and plead with Him. We are His children! We can come boldly before Him as His children and heirs. (Romans 8:14-17, Hebrews 4:14-16)

This does not mean we puff out our chest and begin making demands. Phew! What a stinky attitude! Certainly, an earthly father would not be pleased if their child approached him in that manner.

It is interesting to examine the interaction between us and our Heavenly Father in Hebrews 12:5-11.

There are times our relationship with Jesus includes chastisement. The Greek word for chastisement is "paideuo" which means to train up a child, educate, discipline, chasten, instruct, learn, teach (Holmann's). This is simply part of our relationship with God. He chastens us because He loves us and wants to see us become more and more like Him.

Verse 11 says, "Now no chastening for the present seemeth to be joyous, but grievous: nevertheless afterward it yieldeth the peaceable fruit of righteousness unto them which are exercised thereby."

Do not be discouraged by times of chastening from the Lord. Be encouraged that He loves you enough to chasten you! You are His child and He is shaping you into His image. He loves you too much to let you go down a wrong path.

1 John 4:4 says, "Ye are of God, little children, and have overcome them: because greater is he that is in you, than he that is in the world."

As a Spirit-filled child of God, I can operate in confidence and joy knowing His overcoming power resides within me. What have I to fear? I am a conqueror! (Romans 8:31 and 38-39) I am not overcome by this world or the cares of life, discouragement, or fear. I can operate in the calm confidence that I am His child. Remember, one of the Greek words for joy is "chara" which means "cheerfulness, calm delight, gladness."

Just as there are various ways to interact with others with whom we have relationship, there are multiple ways to interact with our Heavenly Father.

We have already mentioned prayer. Other ways are to read and meditate on His Word (Psalm 1), go to His house (Psalm 27:4), and sing to Him (Psalm 27:6). Find ways to interact with your Father! You will be amazed.

He is our hiding place (Isaiah 32:2). He is our secret place (Psalm 91). We can rejoice in the shadow of His wings (Psalm 63:7).

Isaiah 61:10 "I will greatly rejoice in the Lord, my soul shall be joyful in my God..."

1 Peter 1:8 "Whom having not seen, ye love... ye rejoice with joy unspeakable..."

Perhaps one of the biggest compliments you can give your Heavenly Father is to simply trust in Him. To trust in Jesus is to have joy. Why? Pure trust in Him eliminates joy thieves such as worry and fear.

In need of joy? Purposefully set aside undistracted, uninterrupted time with your Heavenly Father.

"Thou wilt show me the path of life: in thy presence is fullness of joy; at thy right hand there are pleasures for evermore" (Psalm 16:11).

10. Joy Attracts Angels

"Oof!" Daniel landed with a thud.

The dim light began to disappear as a big stone rolled over the opening to the den above him. He quickly checked himself for bruises or broken bones from the fall. There were none.

"Whew!" He sighed with relief, "Thank You, Lord."

Then, he remembered where he was. Weren't lions down here? He stood quietly and let his eyes adjust to the darkness of the lions' den. Meanwhile, he urgently prayed for God's help and protection.

"Lord, if you want me to be supper for these lions just make it as quick and painless as possible!" He shuddered. He thought on how the Lord had delivered his friends out of the fiery furnace. He knew beyond all doubt—if God so chose—He could deliver him out of this situation also. But if not... well, He would see the Lord whom he loved very soon.

Slowly, his eyes adjusted to his surroundings. He heard the sound of soft padded feet around him.

Suddenly, he felt whiskers brush against his cheek! He jumped backward then braced himself for the inevitable. But, nothing happened. What in the world was going on?

He took slow calming breaths between prayers to God for divine intervention.

Then, he saw it. A soft light calmly gliding around the den. Stopping at each beast then moving on to the next one. As he examined the light, he realized he was observing an angel of the Lord. He fell to his knees in relief and thankfulness to God. The angel had shut the lions' mouths!

"Thank You, Lord! Thank You for sending Your angel to my rescue!" His hands were in the air.

Finally, he opened his eyes and looked around him. The lions loafed around occasionally looking at him with hunger and desire but then away as if they knew it was a hopeless cause. They simply could not open their mouths to even get one bite.

"I'm old and tough anyway. You wouldn't have enjoyed me," Daniel chuckled.

Totally relaxed now, he moved toward one of the more serene creatures who was laying on the ground. "Hey buddy. Can't say I'm sorry you missed supper." He peered into the lion's eyes.

"Say, I'm tired. Hold still," He sat down and leaned his head over on the back of the lion's mane.

"Well, Lord, might as well make myself comfortable. I have no idea when the king and his men plan to look down here again."

He yawned and fell into a peaceful sleep.

Daniel had been carried away captive from his homeland of Judah. Then, he was chosen to stand in the enemy king's palace and learn the ways of the heathen. Yet, God brought Daniel into favor with the person placed over him (Daniel 1:9). How could this be if Daniel had chosen to sulk and be upset with his circumstances? No, we see Daniel "purposing in his heart" to continue to live for God even in an enemy nation. His attitude opened a door for God to bring him into favor with those around him.

An attitude of joy creates an atmosphere for angels. What is your attitude attracting?

It is the devil's work to keep us distracted and, therefore, not creating an atmosphere for angelic visitations and angelic presence in our lives.

Daniel had been setting time aside to pray three times a day when God sent an angel to shut the lions' mouths. He had been praying and fasting when God sent an angel in Daniel 9.

"Are they not all ministering spirits, sent forth to minister for them who shall be heirs of salvation?" (Hebrews 1:14)

"There shall no evil befall thee, neither shall any plague come night thy dwelling. For he shall give his angels charge over thee, to keep thee in all thy ways. They shall bear thee up in their hands, lest thou dash thy foot against a stone" (Psalm 91:10-12). If you read the preceding verses, this is referring to people who have made the Lord their refuge and habitation.

When you read 1 Peter 1:12-15, you find that a holy environment attracts angels. Do you maintain an attitude and lifestyle of holiness?

Yes, a joyful attitude no matter what is happening or how you are feeling will attract the angels!

Consider this. What demon would hang around someone who is loving and praising God?

How are you responding to a "bad day?"

One day, I discovered my refrigerator was malfunctioning and I had to turn it off. The next day, I noticed water had leaked from my fridge under the stove. I tried to turn on the stove to cook. It would not work either! What could I do? I had a choice to make. I began to thank God that there was nothing wrong with my coffee pot.

To be honest, I later discovered that when I had unplugged my refrigerator, I had accidentally unplugged my stove also. I had to laugh at myself. Go ahead. You can laugh, too.

If I had chosen to gripe and "lose my joy," what angel would want to be around me?

Be aware of the presence of angels. Make the atmosphere welcoming to them with an attitude of joy. Make room in your life for angelic visitations by weeding out distractions and setting time aside for God.

How much room are you willing to make for the divine? The more room you make, the more joy you will discover in the depths of His presence and in the angelic.

11. Joy Through Worship

The devil tried to keep his composure as he trembled in anticipation. He glanced back again. Yes, Jesus was still there right behind him! Ha!

He and God used to have a great relationship. That was when he was Lucifer, Heaven's worship leader. Oh, yes. He was beautiful and magnificent and musical. Those were the days!

His craving for personal worship had caused him and one third of the angels to get kicked out of Heaven. That had been several thousand years ago. But, now! Opportunity he never dreamed of was playing out before his very eyes.

He quickened his steps as he led Jesus to the top of an exceeding high mountain. His steps began to slow as they reached the top.

He noted how thin and frail the man Jesus looked. The climb had not been easy for Him after forty days of no food. It was so different to see Him this way. So weak. And, hopefully, vulnerable.

He straightened as he began to point out the kingdoms of the world that lay below. How glorious! Worldliness was so attractive to himself. Surely, Jesus would also be impressed just like the rest of mankind.

After finishing his speech, he turned slowly and looked the man in the face. The other two temptations had been nothing compared to this. This was the moment for which he had been waiting!

"All these things will I give thee, if thou wilt fall down and worship me."

After the other two temptations, Jesus had quoted Scripture but had not commanded him to leave. Even after being tempted twice, Jesus had still come with him to this mountain.

Time seemed to stop as the devil held his breath.

"It's always been about the worship," he thought to himself. Before, he had merely sought angelic and human worship for himself. Now, here was his opportunity for God Himself to worship him. That must be what would happen now. Jesus was so very weak and so... human. Humans always made mistakes. He had tricked the first innocent man. Now, he would trick the second one, also!

Jesus straightened His weak human frame and gave the devil a look that made him want to shrivel, "Get thee hence, Satan: for it is written, Thou shalt worship the Lord thy God, and him only shalt thou serve" (Matthew 4:10).

In an instant, Satan left. Disappointment threatened to overcome him. But, Jesus was still a human being. Enraged at yet another lost battle, he roared, "I will kill Him! I will kill Him soon!

Don't you see? It is all about worship.

If Satan would seek to steal worship to himself from the very God of glory robed in human flesh, how much more will he seek to steal your worship? He approached Jesus in perhaps his most weakened human condition outside of Calvary. How much more will he attack you in your weakest moments? How much more will he try to make the world look better than the kingdom of God?

What nerve for the devil to try to get the Holy One to worship him!

And, what nerve he has to approach the children of the King and try to steal their worship.

It is all about the worship. It always has been about worship. Knowing this, it is easy to understand how worship is so powerful.

Can you imagine how the devil reacted when Job fell to the ground and worshipped? Nothing was going right for Job. He had lost everything except his own life. And, his life seemed a miserable existence. Yet Job declared, "Though he slay me, yet will I trust Him!" (Job 13:15)

Satan threw all of his persuasive speeches and accusations against Job to make him question his God and question himself. Yet Job said, "For I know that my redeemer liveth, and that he shall stand at the latter day upon the earth: And though after my skin worms destroy this body, yet in my flesh shall I see God: Whom I shall see for myself, and mine eyes shall behold, and not another; though my reins be consumed within me" (Job 19:25-27).

Satan simply could not steal Job's worship. What happened? Job kept worshipping regardless of Satan's attacks and was doubly blessed in the end.

Are you making the personal application?

Perhaps you are thinking, "But I don't feel joyful when bad things happen to me or life isn't going right!"

Remember, joy is not a feeling. If you have the Holy Ghost, you have joy! (Romans 14:17) You just need to "stir it up" with worship! (2 Timothy 1:6)

When you choose to close your mouth and not worship, you are letting the enemy win the age old battle. But, when you worship regardless of your circumstances, joy will follow. Whether you feel joy or not, rejoice! It is all about worship!

I have wondered in amazement when I read all that people in the Bible went through and yet worshipped. How did they do it? Honestly, many people in the Bible have been through worse things than myself. How can I maintain my joy through worship like they did?

Are you ready for the answer? Here we go…

We were created to worship God. Revelations 4:11 says, "Thou art worthy, O Lord, to receive glory and honour and power: for thou hast created all things, and for thy pleasure they are and were created."

We were not created to live for pleasure, but we were created to live to please our Creator.

Romans 12:1-2 compounds this fact, "I beseech you therefore, brethren, by the mercies of God, that ye present your bodies a living sacrifice, holy, acceptable unto God, which is your reasonable service. And be not conformed to this world: but be ye transformed by the renewing of your mind, that ye may prove what is that good, and acceptable, and perfect, will of God."

Hebrews 11 tells of many people who had obedient faith in God regardless of their circumstances. Verse 17 says, "By faith Abraham, when he was tried, offered up Isaac: and he that had received the promises offered up his only begotten son, Of whom it was said, That in Isaac shall thy seed be called: Accounting that God was able to raise him up, even from the dead; from whence also he received him in a figure."

Abraham lived his life as worship to God. His obedient faith in God was so strong that when God asked him to literally sacrifice the fulfillment of Abraham's promises and dreams, he obeyed. He was willing to offer his son Isaac in worship.

Whoa! Wait a minute! That was really admirable of Abraham, but surely God does not expect that same level of worship from me. Does He?

At the conclusion of a message on this very topic, God's call went out for us to worship Him by sacrificing all of our hopes, dreams, and promises on the altar. If He never fulfilled His promises, if my life never got better, if I lost my health, my family, my hopes, would I still worship Him?

Do I worship God on the basis of what He does for me? Or, do I worship Him because of Who He is? Do I worship God because of His promises? Or, do I worship Him because I love Him?

Dying out to myself and laying my dreams, desires, and wishes on the altar that night was not easy. It was not a service that I left feeling wonderful. Joyful is not an adjective I would have attached to my feelings as I left that night.

66

But, I chose to worship. No matter what. If God never answered another prayer or worked another miracle, I would worship Him and live my life as worship to Him.

As time passed, something began to change in me. It was like the dawning of a new day in my life or the beginning of a new chapter!

I realized that when we take our worship to that level, it plucks a weapon right out of the devil's hands! If the devil comes whispering in our ear that God has not done this or that or fulfilled or whatever... So? Your point? I do not live based on what God does for me. I worship Him because that is what I am created to do and because I love Him! How freeing!

That is the kind of worship the "Heroes Of Faith" had! That is how they could hold on through the worst of trials! That is how the Apostle Paul could stand in the court room falsely accused and wrongly imprisoned and say, "I think myself happy" (Acts 26:2).

That is how the Apostle Paul could boldly stand on the deck of a lost and storm-tossed ship and say, "Sirs, be of good cheer: for I believe God" (Acts 27:25).

Does that mean God will never fulfill His promises? Absolutely not. "God is not a man, that he should lie; neither the son of man, that he should repent: hath he said, and shall he not do it? or hath he spoken, and shall he not make it good?" (Numbers 23:19)

He is the God that cannot lie (Titus 1:2).

However, let me point out that the heroes of faith went through trials that I cannot even begin to imagine. Read Hebrews 11:33-40. These people were tortured, stoned to death, slain with the sword, and much more. "(Of whom the world was not worthy) they wandered in deserts, and in mountains, and in dens and caves of the earth. And these all, having obtained a good report through faith, received not the promise..." (Hebrews 11:38-39).

They still worshipped God even to the death without seeing the promise of God fulfilled in their lifetime! We will stand before God next to these people.

I choose to say, like the Apostle Paul, "Be of good cheer! For, I believe God."

Worship is the most valuable thing in the world. Remember, it is all about worship. From the very beginning, it has always been about worship. If you choose to worship, you are choosing joy.

Do not let your emotions rule! Are you not feeling joy? Stir it up through worship!

It is vitally important to prepare yourself for worship.

Sin separates us from God. Therefore, be quick to repent! All of us make mistakes (Romans 3:23). So, do not be surprised when you mess up. However, do not let the accuser beat you over the head with it! Repent quickly (1 John 1:8-9).

"Create in me a clean heart, O God; and renew a right spirit within me. Cast me not away from thy presence; and take not thy holy spirit from me. Restore unto me the joy of thy salvation; and uphold me with thy free spirit" (Psalm 51:10-12).

Baptism in Jesus' name is a cleansing process a true worshipper must go through.

It is imperative to be filled with the Holy Ghost evidenced by speaking in other tongues. His Spirit living within us guides our choices so that our choices bring worship to God.

If you need further Scripture on repentance, baptism, and the infilling of the Holy Ghost, please review the chapter "Further Revelation Brings Joy."

Then, live a holy life that brings glory to God.

"What? know ye not that your body is the temple of the Holy Ghost which is in you, which ye have of God, and ye are not your own? For ye are bought with a price: therefore glorify God in your body, and in your spirit, which are God's" (1 Corinthians 6:19-20).

"Follow peace with all men, and holiness, without which no man shall see the Lord" (Hebrews 12:14). How can I live a life pleasing to God and in worship to Him if I am not living a holy, separated life?

"Wherefore come out from among them, and be ye separate, saith the Lord, and touch not the unclean thing; and I will receive you, And will be a Father unto you, and ye shall be my sons and daughters, saith the Lord Almighty" (2 Corinthians 6:17-18).

Feed your spiritual man with prayer and the Word of God.

All these things are important to living a life of worship that is acceptable to God.

Truly, this is the best life! This is the joyful life! Pure worship is the key to joy.

Rev. Kim Wood preached a two part message entitled "Hidden In Transparency" and "Transparent Through Pure Worship" in which she shared that pure transparent worship will hide you from the enemy. When you are transparent before God in worship, you are "hidden with Christ in God" (Colossians 3:3).

The best example is Jesus. He was God manifested in the flesh yet "none of the princes of this

world knew: for had they known it, they would not have crucified the Lord of glory" (1 Corinthians 2:8).

How could they not have known? Humility is a covering. Consider the following passage of Scripture regarding Jesus.

"Let this mind be in you, which was also in Christ Jesus: Who, being in the form of God, thought it not robbery to be equal with God: But made himself of no reputation, and took upon him the form of a servant, and was made in the likeness of men: And being found in fashion as a man, he humbled himself, and became obedient unto death, even the death of the cross" (Philippians 2:5-8).

Jesus was transparent. He was open and honest before all. Yet, He was hidden in humility.

There is divine protection and covering in a life humbly lived in pure, untainted worship to God.

In summary, Satan was unsuccessful in stealing the worship of God manifested in the flesh. His attention is now on us. When we

69

have been filled with the Holy Spirit (literally Jesus living in us), Satan continues to try to steal the worship of God to himself.

A true Spirit-filled child of God would not intentionally worship the devil. However, we are always worshipping something. We must be careful to not be distracted (Hebrews 12:1-2) or discouraged from worshipping God. If we stop worshipping God, we turn our worship, energy, time, and focus to something else in God's place. God forbid!

Let us say as Jesus said, "I shall worship the Lord my God, and Him only shall I serve."

12. The Joy Cycle – Soul-Winning

One day, a co-worker commented to me, "Elizabeth, you are always so positive and have a smile. What is your secret?"

"I am filled with the Holy Spirit and walking in relationship with my Heavenly Father," I responded.

My co-worker began to tell of the recent loss of her very religious mother, how she had begun to visit churches, and she concluded with, "...and I hope that when I die I go to heaven."

I began to tell her of a Bible study that I would love to share with her that laid out very plainly in the Scriptures how to get to Heaven. She readily agreed to get with me to learn of these Scriptures.

Hallelujah! I felt joy! Why? I went to work with the joy of the Lord on my countenance and one of my co-workers was drawn to it. Because that co-worker was drawn by the joy of the Lord, she experienced joy. Because she experienced joy through further knowledge and revelation of God's Word, I received joy by seeing a hungry soul embracing more of God. It is the joy cycle in action!

My Pastor, Rev. Roger Wood, said, "God commands us to be happy to show forth His true nature for the sake of others." Therefore, choose joy. Choose to reflect the nature of your Father.

My Pastor also said, "Joy shows the world this is the life."

Let us look more closely into what the Scriptures say about the joy cycle.

Psalm 51:12-13 says, "Restore unto me the joy of thy salvation; and uphold me with thy free spirit. Then will I teach transgressors thy ways; and sinners shall be converted unto thee."

When God restores our joy, we become soul-winners.

We must remember, while we are sowing seeds to water them. "He that goeth forth and weepeth, bearing precious seed, shall doubtless come again with rejoicing, bringing his sheaves with him" (Psalm 126:6).

Water the seeds by shedding tears for the lost in prayer. God says we will "doubtless" be "rejoicing" as we reap the harvest!

Truly, winning a soul to the Lord brings joy to you, to the sinner, and to all of heaven! (Luke 15:3-7)

One night I dreamed that I was at my local church. We were having a service outside and setting up chairs. Joyous music began to waft through the air, and I started to dance in the Spirit. As I danced, a powerful spring of water shot high into the air as if it was coming out of me.

As is typical of springing water, the drops began to splash around me. Some of the drops landed on a nearby prodigal child. She lifted her face toward heaven and began to speak in other tongues.

Still dancing in the Spirit, I saw a family member I have prayed for for many years and started to move in her direction with the springs of water still flowing.

As others started dancing in the Spirit, springs of water shot up from them also.

Wow! What a beautiful dream! Jesus said, "If any man thirst, let him come unto me, and drink. He that believeth on me, as the scripture hath said, out of his belly shall flow rivers of living water. (But this spake he of the Spirit, which they that believe on him should receive...)" John 7:37-39.

When you have the Holy Ghost, you have joy! When you have joy, you are contagious! Spread it around. Spread the joy of the Lord around wherever you go whether you see immediate results or not. Get people wet! "Spring up, O well!" (Numbers 21:17)

As we are joyful witnesses, we must realize that God gives the increase.

I was the Sunday School teacher of the youth class in my church for nearly ten years. I prayed, taught, and did my best to pour the Word into them and to be God's conduit of love.

After church one day, I was standing near the front pew when one of the teens threw her arms wide open and smiled. I smiled at her as she walked right past me into the arms of another lady in the church. Can you imagine how I felt for a moment? I was praying and fasting and teaching her and yet she completely ignored me and went to someone else!

My next thought was, "God, I don't care who in this church they are drawn to as long as they are being won to You."

Has someone you have invited to church one hundred times suddenly shown up with someone else who only invited them once?

I cannot help but laugh here.

Remember that we are all in this soul winning business together. The One Who gives the increase is God. We can all rejoice together when another soul is born into the Kingdom of God! (John 4:35-38)

The Apostle Paul said, "I have planted, Apollos watered; but God gave the increase. So then neither is he that planteth any thing, neither he that watereth; but God that giveth the increase. Now he that planteth and he that watereth are one: and every man shall receive his own reward according to his own labour" (1 Corinthians 3:6-8).

When Paul and Barnabas declared "the conversion of the Gentiles:… they caused great joy unto all the brethren" (Acts 15:3). As we hear of the harvest being reaped in other areas, it produces joy in us!

Then, we go forth into the world manifesting God's joy which then draws more souls to Him. It is a cycle – the joy cycle!

We will not win souls to God if we do not choose to manifest His joy.

One of the recurrent thoughts in the book of Philippians is joy. We continually see the Apostle Paul expressing that the church of Philippi causes him joy. How were they causing him joy? By their "fellowship in the gospel" (Philippians 1:5).

To see a soul continue to grow and mature in the Kingdom of God causes joy in us.

Check out this passage from Philippians 2 verses 14-18. "Do all things without murmurings and disputings: That ye may be blameless and harmless, the sons of God, without rebuke, in the midst of a crooked and perverse nation, among whom ye shine as lights in the world; Holding forth the word of life; that I may rejoice in the day of Christ, that I have not run in vain, neither labored in vain. Yea, and if I be offered upon the sacrifice and service of your faith, I joy, and rejoice with you all. For the same cause also do ye joy, and rejoice with me."

There is a lot of joy happening here! Paul is joyful as he sees those he has won to God shining as lights and holding forth the Word of life. Just seeing them maturing in Christ and being witnesses brings even more joy to him. Paul and the Philippians rejoice together! What a cycle!

As we reap the end time harvest and see multiplication as the harvest wins more souls, what joy! Exceeding joy! It makes every sacrifice and service worth it all.

Paul referred to the Philippians as his "joy and crown" (Philippians 4:1). A source of joy is seeing souls won to God.

Again, in 1 Thessalonians 2:19-20, the Apostle Paul says, "For what is our hope, or joy, or crown of rejoicing? Are not even ye in the presence of our Lord Jesus Christ at his coming? For ye are our glory and joy."

Perhaps I would be amiss if I did not include yet one more verse, "Rejoice in the Lord always: and again I say, Rejoice" (Philippians 4:4).

Soul-winning is not always easy. It requires prayer, sowing, and sacrifice. But be assured that the result of your efforts will be joy. (Psalm 126:6)

"And let us not be weary in well doing: for in due season we shall reap, if we faint not" (Galatians 6:9).

The greatest example we can learn from is that of Jesus Himself. He prayed and sowed and gave into people's lives. Yet, he was rejected, persecuted, and eventually crucified. Did He seem like a successful soul-winner? Yet, every one of us are a result of His sacrifice.

"Looking unto Jesus the author and finisher of our faith; who for the joy that was set before him endured the cross, despising the shame, and is set down at the right hand of the throne of God" (Hebrews 12:2). We were the joy that was set before Him. When Jesus sees us being faithful, being soul-winners, and worshipping Him, it continues to bring Him joy and makes His sacrifice worth it. The joy cycles continues!

I ask again... Did Jesus seem like a successful soul-winner? His ways and His timing are usually different than ours (Isaiah 55:8-11). His timing was perfect as He filled one hundred and twenty souls with His Spirit on the Day of Pentecost! (Acts 2:1-4) Then Peter, a man Jesus had prepared, began to preach and three thousand more souls were born into the kingdom of God (Acts 2:41).

Then in Acts chapter four, five thousand more men believed the salvation message. That is only the beginning.

You see, God did it His way. Do not be discouraged if you do not see immediate results in your soul-winning efforts. Trust God and His timing. Growth will come His way in His timing. God is using us and we will see an end time harvest!

13. The Barometer for Joy (The Word of God)

The year was approximately 445 B.C.

The place – Jerusalem.

Until recently, the great city had lain in ruins. However, God had stirred up the hearts of certain men to return and begin to rebuild this city. First, Zerubbabel had come and led in the rebuilding of the temple. Then, Nehemiah had come and led in the rebuilding of the walls.

Ezra shook his head in amazement as all the people of Jerusalem gathered into the street before him. They had just numbered the people – 42,360. That did not include their servants. All of them were up and ready even though it was morning.

The people had approached Ezra, the scribe, and asked if he would bring out the book of the law of Moses and read it to them. They had prepared a pulpit, or elevated platform, so he could stand above all of the people to be seen and heard as he read the Word.

He continued to watch as the last of the people settled down on the dusty streets. This was a long book. Would they have the patience to hear it?

Now, all eyes were anxiously upon him. He cleared his throat and, reverently, opened the book.

The ground seemed to shake as all the people rose to their feet in honor of the Word.

Ezra wiped a tear from his cheek at the sight and began to bless the LORD.

All the people responded, "Amen! Amen!" They lifted their hands then bowed their heads with their faces to the ground in worship. What a powerful moment!

Finally, with a loud voice so all could hear, he began to read.

All eyes were fixed upon him. Every ear strained to hear. They continued to stand.

As Ezra read, he paused at times to explain what the passages meant.

The sun rose high in the sky. But, the people did not seem to notice so transfixed were they on the holy words being read.

After several hours, Ezra finished and closed the book. As he surveyed the people, many of them wept.

The platform trembled as Nehemiah came up beside Ezra and said, "Mourn not, nor weep. Go your way, eat the fat, and drink the sweet, and send portions unto them for whom nothing is prepared: for this day is holy unto our Lord: neither be ye sorry; for the joy of the LORD is your strength."

A nearly visible wave rippled across the vast crowd. Joy. Pure joy! They began to disperse with laughter and mirth. Why? Because they had understood the words that were declared unto them.

The much loved passage that we quote – "The joy of the LORD is your strength" – came in response to the hearing and understanding of the Word of God in Nehemiah 8.

They were so hungry for the Word of God that they were willing to stand from "morning until midday" (Nehemiah 8:3). And you think your pastor preaches too long?

All Ezra was doing was reading the Word and explaining what it meant. The Bible does not say he was preaching an illustrious, dramatic sermon about a selected verse.

God help us to hunger and thirst for Your Word!

What if you knew of a way to increase your joy? If there was a dollar amount put on joy, how much would you give? If your amount of joy was directly related to how many days you fasted, how long would you fast? If it was directly related to how long you could stand on your head, how long would you do it?

God has given us a spiritual "barometer" for joy. The amount of joy I have is directly related to how much time I am spending intaking the Word of God! I challenge you to try it and see for yourself.

Jesus said, "These things have I spoken unto you, that my joy might remain in you, and that your joy might be full" (John 15:11).

Again, when Jesus prayed in John chapter 17, He said, "...and these things I speak in the world, that they might have my joy fulfilled in themselves" (verse 13).

He has given us His Word that we might be full of joy. Are you seeing the equation? Time in the Word of God equals joy!

Furthermore, the Apostle John wrote, "That which was from the beginning, which we have heard, which we have seen with our eyes, which we have looked upon, and our hands have handled, of the Word of life... These things write we unto you, that your joy may be full" (1 John 1 & 4).

Yet again, His Word is written for us to have joy.

It is simple. Get your Bible, pray for understanding, and start reading. The more you discipline yourself to be in God's Word, the more joy you will have. Get out of your home and to the house of God and listen to the man of God as he preaches the Word. How much joy do you want? Another way to put it is, how much do you want joy?

Since our intake of the Word reflects our amount of joy, then it makes sense that staying in the Word maintains our joy.

How do I stay joyful? How do I keep my joy? Stay in the Word of God. Hunger for His Word.

Pray for a deeper desire for God's Word.

Job said, "I have esteemed the words of his mouth more than my necessary food" (Job 23:12).

Do you want God's Word more than natural food? That is putting it in perspective! However, the result of hungering for God's Word and putting His Word first in our lives is abundant joy.

Let us look at yet another Scripture which verifies this. "Thy words were found, and I did eat them; and thy word was unto me the joy and rejoicing of mine heart" (Jeremiah 15:16).

"The statutes of the LORD are right, rejoicing the heart" (Psalm 19:8).

"I rejoice at thy word, as one that findeth great spoil" (Psalm 119:162).

This is a powerful yet practical way to increase and maintain our joy – intaking the Word of God.

Isaiah 40:8 says, "The grass withereth, the flower fadeth: but the word of our God shall stand for ever." To invest your time in God's Word is a solid investment with increase guaranteed.

"Man shall not live by bread alone, but by every word that proceedeth out of the mouth of God" (Matthew 4:4).

In Leroy Brownlow's book "Better Than Medicine: A Merry Heart," he refers to Matthew 4:4 then says, "A sustenance which nourishes the inward man is essential to peace and happiness" (pg 39).

Read the Word. Speak the Word. Listen to the Word. Obey the Word.

In Acts 8, Philip preached to the people of Samaria. What happened? "And there was great joy in that city" (verse 8). It was important the people of Samaria heard the Word and obeyed it by being baptized in Jesus' Name and receiving the Holy Ghost.

It is important to note that you must couple obedience to the Word with your intake of the Word. "He that keepeth the law, happy is he" (Proverbs 29:18). This has already been covered in the previous chapter "Precedents of Joy."

I would also be remiss if I did not note that joy is not the only benefit of intaking God's Word. Take Psalm 119:165 for example, "Great peace have they which love thy law: and nothing shall offend them." The Word of God is more powerful and beneficial than our human minds can comprehend.

Have you noticed another cycle here? Intaking God's Word equals joy. Joy equals strength. God's Word. Joy. Strength. As God gives you strength, delve into His Word. He blesses you with joy which gives you more strength. This is awesome! This is how God works.

14. Joy Equals Strength

Saul stared in dismay at the fair-faced youthful man who stood before him. He had been so excited and relieved to hear that finally a man had taken the challenge to fight against the Philistine giant! Now, this kid was ushered in to see him. What was his name again? David.

Saul remembered this little guy had been pretty skillful at playing a harp. He even had experience being an armourbearer. What was his occupation? Oh, yes. He watched sheep for his father.

"Let no man's heart fail because of this Philistine. I will go and fight him!" David declared.

Saul sighed and tried to explain, "You are not able to fight against him. You are only a youth, and he has been a man of war from his youth!"

David nodded calmly and replied, "While keeping my father's sheep, a lion and a bear came and took one of the sheep. I went after the sheep and freed it. When the lion came against me, I grabbed him by the beard and killed him. I killed the lion and I killed the bear. It will be the same with this giant because he has defied the armies of the living God!"

Saul stared at the young man. His story was pretty impressive. Maybe, just maybe... "Go, and the LORD be with you."

In an attempt to assist the lad, Saul let him try on his armour. David took it off saying, "I haven't earned these." Then, he left.

Saul watched the unarmed lad leave. Well, he was not completely unarmed. He had noticed the kid carried a slingshot.

David took a deep breath. He had already traveled from his home to the army. Then, he had spoken with the King. Now, he was going to fight a giant. "This is what I would call a busy day," he mused. He had not even had time for a good nap and wholesome meal!

Now, what was his strategy? Ultimately, he trusted that God had delivered him before and God would do it again. Somehow…

A sound caught his attention. Was that the joyful babbling of a brook? David looked around and saw it. An idea popped into his head. He began to search the brook carefully. After picking out five smooth stones, he put them in his pouch.

He had not advanced much closer before it seemed as if the ground began to tremble. "The big brute must stomp for emphasis," David muttered to himself.

David looked toward the giant Goliath. "This is it, Lord. You and me."

Goliath looked around then spotted him. He paused taking him in with a look of surprise then disdain clouded his face. "Am I a dog that you come to me with sticks?" Then, Goliath let out a stream of curses that made David want to put his hands over his ears.

Finally, the giant talked to him like he was a little runt, "Come here. I will give your flesh to the birds of the air and the beasts of the field."

David straightened his back, an anointing and strength flooding his being, "You come to me with a sword, spear, and shield, but I come to you in the name of the LORD of hosts – the God of the armies of Israel, whom you have defied!"

Righteous indignation continued to build as David declared, "This day will the LORD deliver you into my hand. I will kill you. I will take off your head. I will give the carcases of the Philistine army this day to the birds of the air and the wild beasts of the earth that all the earth may know that there is a God in Israel! And, then all these people will know that the LORD does not save with sword and spear, for the battle is the LORD's. He will give you into our hands!"

Goliath's face changed from a look of disdain to utter rage. He let out a roar and ran toward David.

Back in the Israelite camp, Saul shook his head and could hardly bear to watch. David's brothers wondered, "What will we tell our father? How could we let our little brother do this?"

David's eyes never left Goliath as he began to run to meet him. His hand reached into his old pouch and pulled out one of the smooth stones. He put the stone in his trusty slingshot and began to twirl it. He knew God was with him and felt God's strength of which he had often sung filling his being.

With all the strength of God coursing through him, he let the stone go! He watched Goliath's smirking and raging expressions as he thundered toward him. The stone continued its course and hit the giant in the forehead.

Goliath's eyes opened wide in surprised shock! He staggered.

The Israelite and Philistine armies were collectively holding their breath as they watched the giant begin to fall.

David reached the fallen giant and did not waste any time. He was not going to risk the warrior getting back up. He did not stop and feel for a pulse. He reached into Goliath's sheath, pulled out his sword, and with another burst of divine strength, he chopped off his head.

Breathing hard from the exertion, he grabbed his opponents head and lifted it high. He noticed the stone had not just struck him in the forehead, but had broken through the skull and into his head.

Another roar began to rise long and loud over the valley. David looked and saw the Israelite army advancing quickly toward the Philistines. He looked toward the Philistines and saw that they had turned tail and were running away!

David had older brothers who had physical strength and were soldiers in Saul's army. David was viewed as a mere youth with a fair countenance – unfit to be a warrior let alone fight a veteran giant soldier! But, he was the one who had established a relationship with God. He was the one who was writing joyful songs of worship. He had experienced God's strength before and knew God would give him strength again for the challenges ahead.

David wrote, "God is my strength and power: and he maketh my way perfect. He maketh my feet like hinds' feet: and setteth me upon my high places. He teacheth my hands to war; so that a bow of steel is broken by mine arms" (2 Samuel 22:33-35).

Joy and strength are found repeatedly in the Psalms.

"The LORD is my strength and my shield; my heart trusted in him, and I am helped: therefore my heart greatly rejoiceth; and with my song will I praise him. The LORD is their strength, and he is the saving strength of his anointed" (Psalm 28:7-8).

"God is our refuge and strength, a very present help in trouble… There is a river, the streams whereof shall make glad the city of God, the holy place of the tabernacles of the most High" (Psalm 46:1 & 4).

"Sing aloud unto God our strength: make a joyful noise unto the God of Jacob" (Psalm 81:1).

Psalm 16:11 says, "Thou wilt shew me the path of life: in thy presence is fullness of joy; at thy right hand there are pleasures for evermore."

We receive joy from being in the presence of God. And the joy of the Lord is our strength! (Nehemiah 8:10)

When we have spent time in relationship with God, He gives us the power and strength to "tread upon the lion and adder: the young lion and the dragon shalt thou trample under feet" (Psalm 91:1 & 13-14).

There are times I have laughed and told God, "I'm not the energizer bunny!"

Many, if not all of us, face times when we feel tired, worn out, exhausted! It was on such a day that I was praying and telling God I was very tired and still had a busy schedule. The words "The LORD is my light and my salvation; whom shall I fear?" started repeating in my head. I felt impressed to look it up and read it.

I turned to Psalm 27, "The LORD is my light and my salvation; whom shall I fear? the LORD is the strength of my life: of whom shall I be afraid?"

How do I obtain strength? The Scriptures show us that joy and strength come from being in the presence of God and from intaking His Word. Then, the Word tells us that the joy of the LORD is our strength! To have joy is to have strength.

In the same chapter that the Apostle Paul said, "Rejoice in the Lord always: and again I say, Rejoice" (Philippians 4:4), he also declares, "I can do all things through Christ which strengtheneth me!" (Philippians 4:13)

"But the people that do know their God shall be strong, and do exploits" (Daniel 11:32).

Know God. Submit to Him, obey Him, and commit to Him. Spend time in prayer, the Word, and in His house. You will know joy and have his constant strength as you do His work.

Habakkuk 3:17-19 "Although the fig tree shall not blossom, neither shall fruit be in the vines; the labour of the olive shall fail, and the fields shall yield no meat; the flock shall be cut off from the fold, and there shall be no herd in the stalls: Yet I will rejoice in the LORD, I will joy in the God of my salvation. The LORD God is my strength, and he will make my feet like hinds' feet, and he will make me to walk upon mine high places."

Friend, as God gives you joy, He will give you strength. That does not mean you have to be the energizer bunny! God knows when it is time to rest (Example: Genesis 2:1-2). However, He gives us strength in the natural and spiritual that the world does not possess.

When He fills us with His Spirit evidenced by speaking in other tongues, His Spirit gives us a supernatural rest. "For with stammering lips and another tongue will he speak to this people. To whom he said, This is the rest wherewith ye may cause the weary to rest; and this is the refreshing" (Isaiah 28:11-12).

Do not waste the strength He gives you! Spend your time and energy on the work of His kingdom. That is where true joy lies (Romans 14:17).

15. Live with Heaven in view

During one particular church service, we began by singing songs about Heaven. After a couple of songs, our First Lady started on the opposite side of the congregation from where I was sitting and had each individual name something they were looking forward to in Heaven.

Two things immediately popped into my mind and I waited patiently. I listened as one by one people listed the following...

"Streets of gold..."

"The crystal sea..."

"Seeing the face of Jesus..."

"Worshipping around God's throne..."

"Seeing the angels..."

"No more tears..."

"No more sickness..."

"Seeing my loved ones who have died..."

"Ruling and reigning with Christ..."

"The Marriage Supper of the Lamb..."

How wonderful! Finally, my turn came and I said, "Lots of good coffee and a big ping pong table!" The entire congregation burst out laughing. I did not mind.

Yes, I excitedly anticipate all of the above! I do not know how many millenniums it will take before I break away from my Savior and finally check out my mansion. What color will He have made it? What kind of flowers will beautify the landscape? Will I need a coffeepot or just think about it and the perfect cup appear before me? Will raspberry cream chocolates be waiting in my kitchen? Or perhaps cheesecake... And, perhaps in the sitting room there will be the grandest of pianos. Will I even need a bedroom? Naps sure are wonderful on earth… Will I be able to fly?

Imagine never getting tired or sick. Imagine working for Jesus and enjoying every second of it! Imagine no more pain. No more loneliness. No more heartache. No more misunderstandings.

Won't it be wonderful there! It will truly be worth everything we have sacrificed, every prayer, every tear, every trial, and every mile. We have a lot to look forward to!

Knowing this is what the future holds, how can we become discouraged or despondent? Perhaps the next time those feelings come, we should stir up our remembrance of Heaven. And, if we lived in remembrance of what is to come, perhaps those feelings would not happen as often.

We need to be like Jesus in that He looked ahead and did not focus on his current circumstances (Hebrews 12:2). He focused on the "joy that was set before him" and endured. The joy set before us is Heaven. The joy that was set before Him was that we would be joining Him there.

Hebrews 12:3 continues by saying, "For consider him that endured such contradiction of sinners against himself, lest ye be wearied and faint in your minds."

When we are facing opposition from those in the world who do not understand why we live the way we do, remember what Jesus suffered!

And, when "life happens" in all of its ways—sickness, death, heartache, losses, tragedies, accidents—remember, this is not how it all ends.

2 Corinthians 4:16-18 says, "For which cause we faint not; but though our outward man perish, yet the inward man is renewed day by day. For our light affliction, which is but for a moment, worketh for us a far more exceeding and eternal weight of glory; While we look not at the things which are seen, but at the things which are not seen: for the things which are seen are temporal; but the things which are not seen are eternal."

What happens here is temporal. Stay focused on the eternal.

I am not minimizing what we go through. "For we have not an high priest which cannot be touched with the feeling of our infirmities; but was in all points tempted like as we are, yet without sin. Let us therefore come boldly unto the throne of grace, that we may obtain mercy, and find grace to help in time of need" (Hebrews 4:15-16).

Jesus understands what we go through because He has lived as a human and experienced what "life" is like. We can approach Him and discover healing, strength, peace, love, joy, and so much more that is so supernatural—it is divine.

In Matthew 5:10-12 Jesus said, "Blessed are they which are persecuted for righteousness' sake: for theirs is the kingdom of heaven. Blessed are ye, when men shall revile you, and persecute you, and shall say all manner of evil against you falsely, for my sake. Rejoice, and be exceeding glad: for great is your reward in heaven for so persecuted they the prophets which were before you."

Jesus does not miss one thing that we go through. He is watching. He keeps good records. He helps us now and prepares for each of us our eternal reward.

"Lay not up for yourselves treasures upon earth, where moth and rust doth corrupt, and where thieves break through and steal: But lay up for yourselves treasures in heaven, where neither moth nor rust doth corrupt, and where thieves do not break through nor steal: For where your treasure is, there will our heart be also" (Matthew 6:19-21). Set your affection on things above—heaven (Colossians 3:2). While working here below, don't be discouraged if you are not accumulating wealth or seem to be successful. Focus on doing things that have eternal impact! In the long run, that is all that matters.

1 Corinthians 7:31b says, "For the fashion of this world passeth away." Fashion means "circumstance, external condition." Our

current circumstances will not last forever. Our earthly possessions will not last forever.

I was assisting a lady at her home in setting out dishes for company. They were her best and most beautiful dishes which she had been collecting for decades. I accidentally banged a couple of them together and felt immediate chagrin. She calmly said, "Oh, don't worry about it. I won't even need them after the Rapture."

The above example is simple but if we live our life with this perspective, we have a lot more joy and a lot less stress.

It is hard to live in this world because we are not of this world. We are passing through on our journey to Heaven! So, think about your eternal home. Let your mind dwell there. Hum and sing through life and your days the songs about Heaven. It will keep life in its proper perspective.

Following are just a few Scripture passages describing the future of those who are born again and walking in the fullness of Truth.

1 Peter 5:4 "And when the chief Shepherd shall appear, ye shall receive a crown of glory that fadeth not away."

1 Corinthians 15:51-58 "Behold, I shew you a mystery; We shall not all sleep, but we shall all be changed, In a moment, in the twinkling of an eye, at the last trump: for the trumpet shall sound, and the dead shall be raised incorruptible, and we shall be changed. For this corruptible must put on incorruption, and this mortal must put on immortality. So when this corruptible shall have put on incorruption, and this mortal shall have put on immortality, then shall be brought to pass the saying that is written, Death is swallowed up in victory. O death, where is thy sting? O grave, where is thy victory? The sting of death is sin; and the strength of sin is the law. But thanks be to God, which giveth us the victory through our Lord Jesus Christ. Therefore, my beloved brethren, be ye stedfast, unmoveable, always abounding in the work of the Lord, forasmuch as ye know that your labour is not in vain in the Lord."

To have the hope of Heaven takes away the fear or sting of dying. Death is just a gateway from this life into the next. Knowing that we have the ultimate victory through Christ, as long as we are on this earth, steadfastly focus and labor and abound in the work of the Lord! We know beyond doubt that what we do for Jesus will not be in vain—every prayer, every witness, every sacrificial giving of finances or time or energy, every day lived for God is not in vain.

Job 3:17, "There the wicked cease from troubling, and there the weary be at rest."

Revelation 7:9, "After this I beheld, and, lo, a great multitude, which no man could number, of all nations, and kindreds, and people, and tongues, stood before the throne, and before the Lamb, clothed with white robes, and palms in their hands."

Revelation 7:13-17, "And one of the elders answered, saying unto me, What are these which are arrayed in white robes? And whence came they? And I said unto him, Sir, thou knowest. And he said to me, These are they which came out of great tribulation, and have washed their robes, and made them white in the blood of the Lamb. Therefore are they before the throne of God, and serve him day and night in his temple: and he that sitteth on the throne shall dwell among them. They shall hunger no more, neither thirst any more; neither shall the sun light on them, nor any heat. For the Lamb which is in the midst of the throne shall feed them, and shall lead them unto living fountains of waters: and God shall wipe away all tears from their eyes."

Revelation 21:4, "And God shall wipe away all tears from their eyes; and there shall be no more death, neither sorrow, nor crying, neither shall there be any more pain: for the former things are passed away."

As you read these verses, do you feel a longing beginning to stir and build on the inside?

Now, let us take a look at this next verse.

91

Revelation 22:14, "Blessed are they that do his commandments, that they may have right to the tree of life, and may enter in through the gates into the city."

Heaven is a prepared place for a prepared people. Hell is a prepared place for an unprepared people. To be ready for Heaven, we must "do His commandments." We are not just going to "by chance" stumble through the pearly gates. We get to Heaven by doing His commandments—obeying His Word.

I encourage you to obey the Word of God. Remember that as we walk with the Lord, He continues to show us more and more of His Truth. As He reveals more to you, embrace it! It may be more than what your parents or grandparents knew, but it is what He has shown you. What will you do? I urge you to respond with faith and obedience and embrace it. Obey the Word and continue to walk in further revelation. If other people in your life do not understand, perhaps God will use you to guide them into the further revelation. If they choose not to obey themselves, will you still be faithful to your Maker? Will you decide to follow more Truth as He reveals it to you even when others do not understand?

Matthew 16:26-27, "For what is a man profited, if he shall gain the whole world, and lose his own soul? or what shall a man give in exchange for his soul? For the Son of man shall come in the glory of his Father with his angels; and then he shall reward every man according to his works."

In summary, when you live with Heaven in view, you will discover joy. When you live with your focus on Heaven, you will find decision making about the here and now easier.

It is when you seek first the Kingdom of God and His righteousness, that He will take care of all of your earthly needs (Matthew 6:33). Focus on the things of God and what matters in light of eternity. You will discover that Jesus is taking care of the rest.

When I was learning to drive, my driver's education instructor told me, "When young people first start driving, I notice that they tend to look at the road immediately in front of the vehicle. However, you should look up into the distance at the road ahead. That way, you are better prepared and more aware of your surroundings."

The same is true for the road of life. Do not focus on cares that are immediately in front of you, but let your eyes be lifted to the final destination—Heaven.

16. Joy Comes

Is this book making living a joyful life seem easy? The truth is, it is not always easy. Sometimes, choosing joy is an act of obedience. To start singing songs of worship in the middle of chaos or sorrow is not easy. It is the last thing we feel like doing.

Many times I have felt low and thought, "I should start singing." Then, something in me balks and it is hard to think of a song to sing. I will tell myself, "Start singing something!" Once I start lifting up a song of worship, even if it starts out weak, God honors it and begins to shine His light into my darkness.

During the writing of this book, I went through a time where my situations and circumstances of life seemed like they would never change. I knew God had made promises but I could not see a fulfillment anywhere.

Allowing myself to become discouraged, as Elijah before me, I pitifully prayed, "God, if You're ready for me, just take me. I don't want to continue to live down here. Just take me on to Heaven."

Occasionally, I would think, "I've been writing a book about joy. Really? Can I live what God has been moving on me to write? Are the instructions and encouragements of this book doable and effective?"

Then one Sunday, my pastor preached a message entitled "Jesus Is Enough." He preached that we need to be convinced that He is enough. We must be convinced of who we are and what we have inside of us. We are children of God.

He talked about how the devil tries to make us feel guilty like we cannot pray or fast enough. Pastor proceeded to say that the devil had been making some of us feel so discouraged that we just wished we could die. He said this was a trick of the enemy and to give in to such thinking was selfish. Ouch!

As I went to bed that night, I turned on my audio Bible. I awoke in the night thinking on how I had "just wished to die" and what my pastor had said. Suddenly, I became aware of what Scriptures were playing on my audio Bible…

"Moreover all these curses shall come upon thee, and shall pursue thee, and overtake thee, till thou be destroyed; because thou hearkenedst not unto the voice of the LORD thy God, to keep his commandments and his statutes which he commanded thee:

And they shall be upon thee for a sign and for a wonder, and upon thy seed for ever."

Being familiar with the passage, I knew what was coming next and my eyes widened…

"Because thou servedst not the LORD thy God with joyfulness, and with gladness of heart, for the abundance of all things" (Deuteronomy 28:45-47).

I lay in bed now fully awake in stunned silence as the realization that a "God moment" was happening. I looked toward the ceiling and humbly spoke, "Okay, Lord, I get it. I get it."

I fell back asleep and when I awoke in the morning, this passage of Scripture "happened" to be playing…

"…and ye know in all your hearts and in all your souls, that not one thing hath failed of all the good things which the LORD your God spake concerning you; all are come to pass unto you, and not one thing hath failed thereof" (Joshua 23:14).

First, He reminded me of the importance of choosing to serve Him with joy and gladness. Then, He reminded me that His promises always come to pass – not one of them will fail. Hallelujah!

My pastor has said, "Darkness does come into our lives, but it won't last long."

The truth is dark times will come, but we know that joy comes.

"...weeping may endure for a night, but joy cometh in the morning" (Psalm 30:5).

When you read Psalm 30, you see how David extolled and worshipped God in times of prosperity. Then, in the same chapter, he cries to the Lord for help and mercy.

In verse 11 he says, "Thou hast turned for me my mourning into dancing: thou hast put off my sackcloth, and girded me with gladness."

Sackcloth was something worn that meant that person was in a time of sorrow. We have times of sorrow. We have not made it to Heaven yet! However, we can know beyond all doubt that God will always help us and bring us through. Joy will come!

While personally reflecting on all of this, I asked God, "What is the take away from going through this?"

When we have the understanding of what joy really is and the importance of choosing to worship even in dark times, we come to a level of maturity in God. We can keep going knowing Who He is and that joy comes. He is the God of the day and of the night. He "giveth songs in the night" (Job 35:10).

We must look at life with an eternal perspective and not with a temporal perspective.

The Apostle Paul explains it well in 2 Corinthians 4:15-18.

"For all things are for your sakes, that the abundant grace might through the thanksgiving of many redound to the glory of God.

For which cause we faint not; but though our outward man perish, yet the inward man is renewed day by day.

For our light affliction, which is but for a moment, worketh for us a far more exceeding and eternal weight of glory;

While we look not at the things which are seen, but at the things which are not seen: for the things which are seen are temporal; but the things which are not seen are eternal."

Romans 12:12 in the NIV says, "Be joyful in hope, patient in affliction, faithful in prayer."

Remember to be "faithful in prayer." Maintain your altar before God.

No matter what you are going through or how you are feeling, remember... Joy comes.

Truthfully, joy is always present. But, we do not always feel it. Remember that to be filled with the Spirit of God is to be filled with joy.

Remember the analogy in the beginning of this book of a classic musical piece? Maybe you are going through a low, minor time but a crescendo into a joyous rapture is about to happen.

Why do we go through hard times? 2 Corinthians 4:8-9 says, "We are troubled on every side, yet not distressed; we are perplexed, but not in despair; persecuted but not forsaken; cast down, but not destroyed."

True. There are troubles and distresses and persecutions. But, why? Let us see what the next two verses reveal...

"Always bearing about in the body the dying of the Lord Jesus, that the life also of Jesus might be made manifest in our body. For we which live are always delivered unto death for Jesus' sake, that the life also of Jesus might be made manifest in our mortal flesh" (vs 10-11).

We go through things that Jesus might be manifested through us! Wow!

See, Jesus' body was broken for us. Therefore, we experience brokenness also. When we become broken before God (not bitter – broken), we allow "self" (our carnal nature) to be emptied out. When we are empty of "self" and are transparent before Him, He can shine through us.

Then, when the world looks on us, they do not just see a "happy" person. They see the joy that God brings in the midst of brokenness—in the midst of life. It makes them want what we have.

Hard times and tragedies will happen to everyone. That is the result of sin. God made the world perfect but then came sin. With sin came carnality, disease, death, etc. When it happens to you, will you be bitter or bring your brokenness to God?

Psalm 51:8 and 17 says, "Make me to hear joy and gladness; that the bones which thou hast broken may rejoice… The sacrifices of God are a broken spirit: a broken and a contrite heart, O God, thou wilt not despise."

Remember, you will never know the fullness of joy until you have experienced sorrow.

God allows things to happen in our lives that break us. When we come before God and pour out ourselves to Him, His joy and character shines through us.

What is so amazing about our God is that He takes the awful, sorrowful things we are going through and, when we continue in obedience and submission to Him and His Word, He makes "all things work together for good" (Romans 8:28).

Let us wrap up this chapter with the following verse, "Now the God of hope fill you with all joy and peace in believing, that ye may abound in hope, through the power of the Holy Ghost" (Romans 15:13).

17. The Health Benefits

I have been a nurse since 2005 and have had many experiences throughout the years. Please allow me to share a couple of them with you.

The second shift nurse thoroughly shared with me the details of how her evening caring for "Ms. Lena" (name changed to protect the HIPPA laws) had gone. "Terrible! She constantly complains of being in pain, she won't get up and walk, and she argues about her medications. She is treating all of the staff rudely. I don't know how you're going to deal with her tonight."

I listened quietly writing down the appropriate report and mentally absorbing the disposition of this postoperative patient.

The mentally exhausted second shift nurse finished her report and went home. I am accustomed to such reports as our world is full of hurting people with all kinds of personalities, life experiences, and behavioral difficulties. I breathed a silent prayer for God's help and walked into Ms. Lena's room.

I put my best Holy Ghost-filled smile on and began to interact with her and do my assessment. I gave her medication to relieve her pain. I listened to her talk about how awful she felt after surgery.

Finally, our conversation turned to where she lived, how she loved to cook, and her passion for art. At last, I offered to pray with her. She readily accepted and we joined hands and prayed.

The next night, I got report on Ms. Lena from the same second shift nurse. "I don't know what happened but Ms. Lena is completely different. It's like she's not the same person. She's been so nice, joking with the staff, and walking in the halls…"

Another time I was working day shift. I received report on a young man caught up in drugs. He was admitted because he had attempted to commit suicide. He had to stay until a psychiatrist came and evaluated him.

I began to do my nursing duties like normal but I could see the pain and hurt in his eyes and facial expression. He felt defeated. He felt low and depressed. He did not know how he was going to handle another day of life.

Finally, I stood by his bedside and asked, "May I pray for you?"

His eyes lit up, "I knew you were a Christian! I could tell. There was something different about you."

He allowed me to pray. I prayed as the Holy Spirit directed me. When I finished, he clasped my hand with both of his and with tears in his eyes said, "Thank you. You've given me my life back."

I told him that Jesus was the One he was to thank.

Afterwards, the psychiatrist came, evaluated him, and decided he was okay to be released.

I have interacted with many people on a very broad spectrum ranging from those with anxiety to the severely depressed to the suicidal. I have been the nurse of many patients who simply came into the hospital thinking they had a treatable pain and were told they had terminal cancer. How do you deal with it? What is the answer?

The medical field has come a long way in different kinds of medications that treat and help improve the symptoms of organic mental disorders. There are people that testify of various medications that have improved their symptoms of depression and anxiety.

Also, many therapies are promoted such as counseling, meditation, exercise, proper rest, a healthy diet, doing things you enjoy such as hunting, fishing, golfing, crafts, etc. There is teaching on how to avoid or how to handle emotional triggers.

I am not an authority on these things but have been exposed to this information throughout my medical career.

One night, I was pulled from my home department to the Emergency Room. My job was to make sure a confused lady who had broken her hip stayed on the ER bed and did not hurt herself further. The ER was so full that every room was occupied plus patients were sitting on chairs in the hallway with little portable dividers between them. There were more people still needing attention in the waiting room.

As I kept watch over my assigned patient, I overhead a young man's voice telling his ER nurse, "I'm so anxious. I can't sleep. I need help."

The ER nurse, "Did you try doing something that relaxes you?"

"Yes. I tried playing video games. I tried listening to music. I am just so nervous. I can't handle it! Nothing works. I need something to calm me down," the young man explained anxiously.

The ER nurse, "What do you want?"

"Could I just have a shot of Ativan?"

"You know that's not going to help you in the long run," the ER nurse responded without sympathy. You see, these front line staff see such cases so many times that it becomes hard to feel compassion or empathy.

The young man implored, "I know, but it helps me calm down then maybe I can get some rest."

"Okay. I'll go talk to the doctor," the ER nurse walked off.

While waiting on the nurse to return, I could tell the young man was discussing his difficulties with another person who had come with him.

On the inside, I wanted to go talk with the young man, to pray with him, to offer him hope. But, I dutifully kept my attention on the pleasantly forgetful lady who could not remember where she was and barely knew who she was let alone that she had a broken femur.

After some time, the ER nurse returned, "I have an Ativan pill for you. You can take it then stay here until we know it has begun to work. Then, you may be dismissed but we strongly recommend you spend time meditating, talking to your Higher Power, eat properly, and participate in hobbies that you enjoy."

101

"Yes, ma'am. Thank you," he took the pill.

The ER nurse walked away and I could not take it any longer. I looked at my charge who was snoring softly. Then, stepped around the partition, looked at the anxious young man, and asked, "May I say a prayer with you?"

He looked surprised but was agreeable. I stood there and prayed over him, prayed that he would have peace and God's help in his life and in his future. When I finished, he sincerely thanked me.

It is true in every area of the medical field—we have limitations. We have come a long way but there is only so far that we can go in our efforts to heal. But, there is One Who has no limitations—God.

He can not only heal the body but He can heal the mind and the broken spirit. He can heal emotions and heartaches.

A disturbed gentleman was on my medical floor one night. When I offered to pray with him, he angrily said, "No! My little girl died. I don't believe in a God who would let that happen."

I calmly bent by his bed and began to explain, "When God made this world, He made it perfect. There was no disease, no dying, and no wrong doing. Then, man chose to sin. With sin came disease, the death process, and all the hurt. But, it is God Who came down as a human and took the stripes on His back for our healing, Who died on the cross to pay the penalty for our sins, and Who wants to be our Comforter and help us get to Heaven."

The gentleman who had been volatile and angry before, now lay quietly absorbing this new information. I said my own silent prayers for him as I slipped away.

Colossians 2:10 says, "And ye are complete in him." God made us with a part that only He can fill.

Leroy Brownlow describes that we must live our lives around a great center—God (Better Than Medicine: A Merry Heart, pg. 40). When He is at the center of our lives, He holds us together and keeps us from falling to pieces. And, when life is full of troubles and woes, we can lift up our eyes to Jesus and be able to see above the problems (Psalm 121).

He also refers to the following quote by Jung (pg. 64). "Side by side with the decline of religious life, the neuroses grow noticeably more frequent."

This is true. Without God, neurotic diseases increase. Why? Remember, we are complete in Him. It is not until we are in right relationship with Jesus that we have completeness.

Here is another thought from 1 Peter 3:10-11, "For he that will love life, and see good days, let him refrain his tongue from evil, and his lips that they speak no guile: Let him eschew evil, and do good; let him seek peace, and ensue it."

Interesting that we see the admonition to guard our tongue! (Remember: What are you calling forth?)

Furthermore, if you will love life and have good days, avoid evil and do good. Seek peace and pursue it. Do what is right. Follow peace.

Do you want joy? Follow peace. Do not choose to do things that prick your conscience or that you know will have bad outcomes. As you walk with God, do not involve yourself in sinful pleasures. Do not entangle yourself with worldliness. But, do good and follow peace.

Lastly, let us look again at 2 Corinthians 4:8-9, "We are troubled on every side, yet not distressed; we are perplexed, but not in despair; Persecuted, but not forsaken; cast down, but not destroyed."

Leroy Brownlow responds to the above passage with, "Whatever it was that kept this man from distress, despair and destruction, is what all of us want, for every life has its own troubles" (pg. 48).

He later describes the answer as positive thinking (pg. 53).

Friend, let me tell you what the Apostle Paul who wrote the above had! He had repented of his sins, been baptized by immersion in Jesus' name, and had received the infilling of the Holy Ghost evidenced by speaking in other tongues. He was walking in right relationship with God day by day submitted, obedient, and fully committed to Him and His leadership in his life.

Acts 1:8 says, "But ye shall receive power, after that the Holy Ghost is come upon you."

When you are filled with the Holy Ghost, you have the power of the Almighty God resident inside of you. When you have been baptized in Jesus' name, you have the authority of the family name applied to your life. Therefore, you can walk submitted, obedient, and committed to God. Then, life can hit but it will not destroy you. Things may get confusing but it will not put you in despair or depression. You just keep your eyes on Jesus and He will guide you through to the other side.

18. Maintaining Your Joy

While getting ready to start another day, I was talking with Jesus. There were many needs to pray about. These needs were not for myself but for others. I wondered aloud to God, "How can I have joy when there is so much to pray about? People are sick, homes are being wiped out and lives lost through natural disasters, children are being neglected and abused, there is political upheaval, and the list goes on. How can I pray about all this and still be joyful?"

I almost felt guilty to feel happiness or have joy when I felt such an awareness of all these things.

Thoughts of Peter walking on the water amidst the storm came to my mind. He was walking on stormy waters with the storm raging around him. Yet, as long as he kept his eyes on Jesus, he would not sink. However, when he turned his focus to the storm around him, he immediately began to sink. Even when he got out of focus, he called out to Jesus who was right there to lift him back up.

I said, "Okay, Lord, I get it. I can pray about these things and leave them to You. Then, keep my eyes on You and not worry about all of them and still walk in joy."

The following song came to mind and I began to sing…

"Turn your eyes upon Jesus.

Look full in His wonderful face,

And the things of this earth will grow strangely dim,

In the light of His glory and grace."

By Helen H. Lemmel, 1922

How do you maintain your joy? Walk with Jesus. Embrace His Word as He reveals more and more to you. Keep a right attitude and spirit (Psalm 51:10). Be sure you are submitted, obedient, and committed to Him.

Be careful what you are thinking and what you are feeding into your mind. Then, do not complain. Speak positive. Speak God's promises and truths. Speak thanks.

My pastor occasionally tells us new words. One of these is "Thanksliving." Live a life of thanks!

Watch out for joy thieves!

Remember to enjoy the journey. Learn to laugh! Smile! "A merry heart doeth good like a medicine" (Proverbs 17:22).

Stay in relationship with your Heavenly Father. Prioritize prayer. Interact with Him. Get to know Him.

Remember that a joyful attitude attracts the angels. Create an atmosphere through your attitude, singing, worship, speaking, cheerfulness, and kindness to others that invites the angels.

If you have the Holy Ghost, you have joy. If you have God, you have joy! If you do not feel it, stir it up! Worship! Sing! Speak aloud, "Spring up, O well!" (Numbers 21:17, John 7:37-39)

Be a soul winner. Get out of yourself. Reach for others. Give your best and the best will come back to you.

Remember the barometer for joy is the Word of God. Keep reading the Bible! Read it daily. The amount of the Word of God you intake is directly related to your amount of joy. Conversely, you cannot omit the intaking of the Word of God and expect to have joy.

Remember that joy equals strength. The joy of the Lord is our strength.

When life gets rough and you do not feel the joy, remember that it is not a feeling. It is a choice. But, that feeling of joy will come again—assuredly.

Live your life always focused on your ultimate destination—Heaven. Invest in the eternal. As is commonly said, "Don't sweat the small stuff."

Walk in the Spirit. Stay filled with His Spirit. Keep Him as the center of your life and you will not unravel or become fragmented in your mind.

Do not let yourself be offended in God. Do not become upset with your Maker when life is not how you planned or thought it would be. This will drain your joy faster than anything. Joy Haney said in her book "Diamonds For Dusty Roads," "We choose our destiny by our attitude towards God" (pg. 450).

Stay faithful to God and to the man of God He has put in your life.

Come to God's house faithfully! He promises to "...make them joyful in my house of prayer" (Isaiah 56:7).

Can you make the transition from feelings to choice? You must be intentional. It is an intentional change of mindset to live joyfully.

"Let us hear the conclusion of the whole matter: Fear God, and keep his commandments: for this is the whole duty of man" (Ecclesiastes 12:13).

To have a respectful fear of God and to obey His Word will maintain your joy.

Jesus said, "And now I come to thee; and these things I speak in the world, that they might have my joy fulfilled in themselves."

In the midst of a world that is darker than ever before and full of calamity, God is desiring to restore joy in an unprecedented manner. He wants His children to walk in true joy as He originally intended. He wants to restore old-fashioned, Spirit-filled joy in this end time.

Our sin-darkened world is hungering for joy and completeness. As we walk in the fullness of His joy, we will brightly shine! We have the answer for which they are hungering and thirsting.

Walk humbly before Him in pure, transparent worship. Walk in relationship with your Heavenly Father. Bask in His love, and He will keep you overflowing with joy.

Made in USA - Kendallville, IN
52849_9798840752999
07.27.2022 0755